Mastering the New York Intermediate-Level Social Studies Test

DeHollander • Morrison • Schockow • Sesso

Mc Graw Hill **Glencoe**

New York, New York   Columbus, Ohio   Chicago, Illinois   Peoria, Illinois   Woodland Hills, California

Send all inquiries to:
Glencoe/McGraw-Hill
8787 Orion Place
Columbus, OH 43240

ISBN 0-07-868881-7

Printed in the United States of America

7 8 9 10 108 09 08

TEACHER REVIEWERS

Credits

TABLE OF CONTENTS

Unit 10—The Role of the United States in the World, *1939–1990*

Unit 11—The American People in a Changing World, *1950–Present*

CORRELATION CHART

Correlation of Practice Test Questions to the New York State Core Curriculum for Social Studies

New York Core Curriculum for Grade 8	Test 1	Test 2	Test 3	Test 4	Test 5	Test 6
Unit One: The Global Heritage of the American People Prior to 1500						
I. History and the Social Sciences: The Study of People	I, 2–3, 7–12, 15–16, 19–21; IIA, 1					
II. Geographic Factors Influence Culture	I, 1, 4, 13–14, IIA, 2–3; IIB, 4–6					
III. Iroquoian and Algonquian Cultures on the Atlantic Coast of North America	I, 5–6, 17–18	IIA, 1–2				
IV. European Conceptions of the World in 1500	IIIA, 1–3, IIIB	I, 1–3, 6–8, 14, IIA, 3				
Unit Two: European Exploration and Colonization of the Americas						
I. European Exploration and Settlement		I, 1–2, 4, 5, 9, 10, 11, 12, 13, 15–18, 32; IIIB				
II. Colonial Settlement: Geographic, Political, and Economic Factors		I, 18–27, 30–31, 33–34, 36–37	I, 2			
III. Life in Colonial Communities		I, 28–29, 35, 38; IIB, 1–3; IIIA, 1–3, IIIB	I, 4–5			
Unit Three: A Nation I Created						
I. Background Causes of the American Revolution			I, 1–4, 7–19, 25; IIIA, 1, 3; IIIB			
II. The Shift From Protest to Separation			I, 6, 20–21, 31, 35–37; IIIA, 1–3; IIIB			
III. Early Attempts to Govern the Newly Independent States			I, 6, 22–23, 26–27; IIA, 1–3	I, 1; IIIA, 1–2; IIIB		
IV. Military and Political Aspects of the Revolution			I, 24, 28–30, 32–34, 39–42; IIB, 1–2			
V. Economic, Political, and Social Changes Brought about by the American Revolution			I, 38	I, 3–4, 20–21; IIB, 1–3		
Unit Four: Experiments in Government						
I. The Articles of Confederation and the Critical Period				I, 1, 10, 12–13; IIA, 1–3; IIIA, 3; IIIB		
II. The New York State Constitution of 1777				I, 6		
III. The Writing, Structure, and Adoption of the United States Constitution				I, 5–9, 11–19, IIA, 1–3		
Unit Five: Life in the New Nation						
I. New Government in Operation				I, 22–26, 28	I, 1–19, 27	
II. The Age of Jackson				I, 27	I, 31–37, 39–46, 49; IIA, 1–3; IIB, 1–3	
III. Preindustrial Age: 1790–1860s				I, 2, 20–21	I, 20–26, 38, 46–48, 50–63; IIIA, 1–3; IIIB	
Unit Six: Division and Reunion						
I. Underlying Causes of the Civil War				I, 4	I, 29–30, 40, 59–60, 65–66	I, 1–19, 21, 26–27; IIA, 1–3; IIB, 1–3
II. The Civil War Breaks Out						I, 20, 22–26, 28–33, 35–39
III. Results of the Civil War						I, 34, 36, 40–47; IIIA, 1–3; IIIB

New York Core Curriculum for Grade 8	Test 7	Test 8	Test 9	Test 10	Test 11
Unit Seven: An Industrial Society					
I. The Maturing of an Industrial Society in the Second Half of the 19th Century	I, 1–7, 10, 15, 20–31	IIIA, 1–3; IIIB			
II. Changes in the Social Structure Altered the American Scene	I, 8–9, 11–14, 16–20, 31, 38–42, 44; IIA, 1–3; IIB, 1–3				
III. The Progressive Movement, 1900–1920: Efforts to Reform the New Society	I, 32–37, 43, 45–55; IIIA, 1–3; IIIB	I, 11; IIA, 1–2; IIIA, 2; IIIB			
Unit Eight: The United States as an Independent Nation in an Increasingly Interdependent World					
I. The United States Expands its Territories and Builds an Overseas Empire		I, 2–5, 7, 9–10, 12–13, 15, 18; IIB, 1–3			
II. The United States Begins to Take a Role in Global Politics		I, 1, 6, 8, 14, 16–17, 19–34			
Unit Nine: The United States Between the Wars					
I. The Roaring Twenties Reflected the Spirit of the Postwar Period			I, 1–6, 8–14; IIA, 1–3; IIB, 1–3		
II. The Great Depression			I, 15–28; IIB, 1–3; IIIA, 1–3; IIIB	I, 1	
Unit Ten: The United States Assumes Worldwide Responsibilities					
I. World War II			I, 7	I, 1–20; IIA, 1–3	
II. The United States as Leader of the Free World				I, 21–22, 24, 26–31, 35–36, 38–48, 50–51, 55–57; IIIA, 1–3; IIIB	IIA, 2–3; IIIB
III. The United States in the Post-Cold War World				I, 49, 57; IIB, 1–3; IIIA, 3' IIIB	I, 24–32, 37
Unit Eleven: The Changing Nature of the American People From World War II to the Present					
I. Postwar Society Characterized by Prosperity and Optimism				I, 23, 25, 32–34, 37, 52–54, 56	I, 1–23, 33–36; IIA, 1–3; IIB, 1–3; IIIA, 2–3; IIIB
II. The United States Begins a New Century				IIIA, 3; IIIB	I, 38–40; IIA, 1–3

TAKING THE NEW YORK INTERMEDIATE-LEVEL SOCIAL STUDIES TEST

This book is set up to help you prepare for the New York Intermediate-Level Social Studies Test. The book is divided into two main sections. First, you will find 14 *Skillbuilders* review lessons and worksheets. These pages will help you review the critical thinking and social studies skills that you will need to analyze many of the questions on the test.

The remainder of the book contains practice test questions like the ones that you will be given in the exam. It is set up in the same order as your social studies textbook. In every unit, you will practice answering three types of questions: multiple-choice questions, constructed-response questions, and document-based questions.

Before you begin, read these strategies to help you answer each type of question.

MULTIPLE-CHOICE QUESTIONS

1. Read the question carefully to make sure you understand what is being asked. Pay attention to key words in the question like *BEST, MAIN, MAJOR, ONLY,* and *ALL.*

2. Read *all* of the answer choices. Cross out any choice that you know is incorrect or that is not related to the question. Remember that an answer choice may make a statement that is true but does not relate to or answer the question being asked.

3. Reread the remaining choices. Keep in mind that you may not find a perfect choice. In this case, choose the answer that you think *best* answers the question.

4. Be aware that answers containing words like *all, every,* and *totally* are usually incorrect because these words over-generalize. Correct answers often include words like *some, often, many,* or *generally.*

5. Questions are usually presented in chronological order. Knowing that might help you choose the correct answer or eliminate those obviously outside the time period.

The constructed-response and document-based questions in the New York Intermediate-Level Social Studies Test are based on written and visual documents, such as journal entries, speeches, cartoons, graphs, and maps.

CONSTRUCTED-RESPONSE QUESTIONS

1. Identify the type of document presented. Always read the caption; it will provide valuable information about the document.

2. Read the three questions that follow the document.

3. As you read or study the document, underline or identify in some other way any information that will help you answer the questions.

4. Refer to information from the document in your answers.

DOCUMENT-BASED QUESTIONS

1. Read the introduction to the activity. Then read the historical context and the task.

2. Read or study each document. Underline or identify in some other way any information that will help you answer the essay question.

3. Answer the short-answer questions that follow the document.

4. After you have read all the documents and answered all the short-answer questions, read the essay question again.

5. Write a sentence or two that summarizes your answer to the essay question. Then outline your essay. Note how you can use the documents to support your answer. Remember, you do not have to include every document in your answer.

6. Include additional outside information. It may be helpful to brainstorm a list of additional outside information that will be useful and relevant to your answer.

7. Write your essay. Make sure you include an introduction, several paragraphs, and a conclusion. Support your response with relevant facts, examples, and details.

8. Edit your essay. Make sure your sentences are clearly written. Correct any spelling and punctuation errors.

DOCUMENT-BASED SCORING RUBRIC

From the Revised Generic Scoring Rubric for Regents Examinations.

Score of 5:
- Thoroughly develops all aspects of the task evenly and in depth
- Is more analytical than descriptive (applies, analyzes, evaluates, and/or creates information)
- Incorporates relevant information from *at least* the requested number of documents
- Incorporates substantial relevant outside information
- Richly supports the theme with many relevant facts, examples, and details
- Demonstrates a logical and clear plan of organization; includes an introduction and a conclusion that are beyond a restatement of the theme

Score of 4:
- Develops all aspects of the task but may do so somewhat unevenly
- Is both descriptive and analytical (applies, analyzes, evaluates, and/or creates information)
- Incorporates relevant information from *at least* the requested number of documents
- Incorporates relevant outside information
- Supports the theme with relevant facts, examples, and details
- Demonstrates a logical and clear plan of organization; includes an introduction and a conclusion that are beyond a restatement of the theme

Score of 3:
- Develops all aspects of the task with little depth *or* develops most aspects of the task in some depth
- Is more descriptive than analytical (applies, may analyze and/or evaluate information)
- Incorporates some relevant information from some of the documents
- Incorporates limited relevant outside information
- Includes some relevant facts, examples, and details; may include some minor inaccuracies
- Demonstrates a satisfactory plan of organization; includes an introduction and a conclusion that may be a restatement of the theme

Score of 2:
- Minimally develops all aspects of the task *or* develops some aspects of the task in some depth
- Is primarily descriptive; may include faulty, weak, or isolated application or analysis
- Incorporates limited relevant information from the documents *or* consists primarily of relevant information copied from the documents
- Presents little or no relevant outside information
- Includes few relevant facts, examples, and details; may include some inaccuracies
- Demonstrates a general plan of organization; may lack focus; may contain digressions; may not clearly identify which aspect of the task is being addressed; may lack an introduction and/or a conclusion

Score of 1:
- Minimally develops some aspects of the task
- Is descriptive; may lack understanding, application, or analysis
- Makes vague, unclear references to the documents *or* consists primarily of relevant and irrelevant information copied from the documents
- Presents no relevant outside information

- Includes few relevant facts, examples, or details; may include inaccuracies
- May demonstrate a weakness in organization; may lack focus; may contain digressions; may not clearly identify which aspect of the task is being addressed; may lack an introduction and/or a conclusion

Score of 0: Fails to develop the task or may only refer to the theme in a general way; *OR* includes no relevant facts, examples, or details; *OR* includes only the historical context and/or task as copied from the test booklet; *OR* includes only entire documents copied from the test booklet; *OR* is illegible; *OR* is a blank paper

Skillbuilder 1: Understanding Cause and Effect

A *cause* is a person, place, event, or condition that makes something happen. What happens as a result is an *effect*.

Understanding this skill will help you answer questions such as the one shown below. Follow the steps to practice the skill. Then, answer the question on the line provided.

1. Identify two or more events.
2. Ask questions about why the events occur.
3. Look for clue words such as *because, led to, brought about, produced,* and *therefore.*
4. Identify the outcome of the events.
5. Write the number of the best answer on the line below.

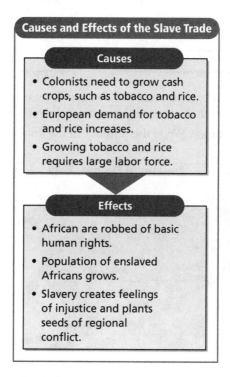

Causes and Effects of the Slave Trade

Causes
- Colonists need to grow cash crops, such as tobacco and rice.
- European demand for tobacco and rice increases.
- Growing tobacco and rice requires large labor force.

Effects
- African are robbed of basic human rights.
- Population of enslaved Africans grows.
- Slavery creates feelings of injustice and plants seeds of regional conflict.

_____ **According to the information in the chart, which of the following statements is accurate?**

(1) The slave trade led to the colonists' need to grow more cash crops.
(2) Because the population of enslaved Africans grew, a large labor force was required to grow tobacco and rice.
(3) Europeans demanded more tobacco and rice because Africans were robbed of basic human rights.
(4) The development of the slave trade created feelings of injustice and planted seeds of regional conflict.

Skillbuilder 2: Reading a Special-Purpose Map

Maps that show information on specialized subjects, or themes, are called special-purpose maps. They differ from general-purpose maps in that they show more than basic physical features or political boundaries. Special-purpose maps can contain physical, economic, climatic, historic, or cultural information—almost anything that can be expressed geographically.

Understanding this skill will help you answer questions such as the one shown below. Follow the steps to practice the skill. Then, answer the question on the line provided.

1. Read the map title and labels to determine the subject and purpose of the map.
2. Study the map key or legend. Identify each symbol and color, shade, or pattern in the key and locate these on the map.
3. Use this information to look for similarities and differences in the region shown.
4. Write your conclusion(s) about what is shown on the map.

_____

_____

5. Read the question. Check each answer choice against your own conclusion to see if they agree. Then check each answer choice against the information on the map.
6. Select the best answer choice. Write the number of the answer choice on the line.

Presidential Election, 2000

	Electoral Vote (270 to win)	Popular Vote
☐ Al Gore	266	50,996,164
■ George W. Bush	271	50,456,169
10 Number of state electoral votes		
*1 elector from Washington, D.C., abstained.		

_____ **According to the map, which statement is true?**

(1) Al Gore won the popular vote.
(2) Texas had more electoral votes than California.
(3) Al Gore won the election.
(4) George Bush won fewer electoral votes than Al Gore did.

Skillbuilder 3: Identifying the Main Idea

Historical details, such as names, dates, and events, are easier to remember when they are connected to a main idea. The main idea of a passage is its central, or most important, issue.

Understanding this skill will help you answer questions such as the one shown below. Follow the steps to practice the skill. Then, answer the question on the line provided.

1. Read the passage. Determine the topic discussed in the passage. What is the topic discussed in the passage below?

_____

_____

2. Identify important details that support the topic being discussed.
3. Identify the main idea or central issue. The main idea may be stated directly or it may be implied, or stated indirectly.
4. Read the question. Write the number of the best answer on the line.

> A person who has dual citizenship claims citizenship in two countries. He or she is obliged to obey the legal requirements of citizenship of both countries. To avoid problems, a person who is or plans to become a dual citizen needs to know the laws of both countries. In some cases, the person may automatically lose citizenship in one country upon becoming a citizen of the other. The dual citizen will likely need separate passports for entering or leaving each country. Both countries may require the dual citizen to pay taxes or serve in the military.

_____ **Which statement BEST expresses the main idea of the passage above?**

(1) Many people choose to become citizens of two countries.
(2) The dual citizen has to obey the legal requirements of both countries.
(3) It is easy to become a citizen of two countries.
(4) The dual citizen may have to pay taxes in both countries.

Skillbuilder 4: Reading Graphs

Information can be presented in bar graphs, line graphs, or circle graphs. A circle graph, sometimes called a pie chart, is most useful for showing parts of a whole. If you show several circle graphs together, they can be used to show changes over time.

Understanding this skill will help you answer questions such as the one shown below. Follow the steps to practice the skill. Then, answer the question on the line provided.

1. Study the labels or key to identify what each part of the circle represents.
2. Compare the individual parts of the graph to draw conclusions about the subject.
3. If two or more circle graphs appear together, read their titles and labels.
4. Compare the graphs for similarities and differences.
5. Write the number of the best answer on the line below.

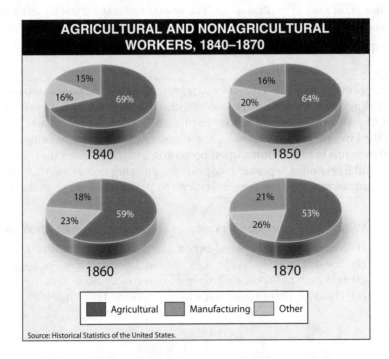

Source: Historical Statistics of the United States.

_____ **Which statement about agricultural and nonagricultural workers is supported by the graphs?**

(1) Between 1840 and 1870, there were always more workers in manufacturing than in agriculture.

(2) There were no workers in agriculture in 1860.

(3) In 1840, the dotted section of the graph represents the greatest percentage of workers.

(4) The greatest decrease in the percentage of agricultural workers occurred between 1860 and 1870.

Skillbuilder 5: Making Inferences and Drawing Conclusions

Making inferences and drawing conclusions allows you to understand ideas that are not stated directly. When you make an inference, you make a decision based on your observations and knowledge. When you draw conclusions, you might use several inferences or facts to make a decision.

Understanding this skill will help you answer questions such as the one shown below. Follow the steps to practice the skill. Then, answer the question on the line provided.

1. Determine the topic of the question.
2. Read the passage. Focus on the facts, or what you know to be true.
3. Recall information or facts you might have acquired from reading about related topics or observing similar situations.
4. Pay close attention to the details. They can indicate facts that are not stated.
5. Keeping the question in mind, decide what you can infer from the passage. Write your inference here.

_____

_____

_____

6. Check each answer choice against your own inference to see if they agree.
7. Select the best answer choice. Write the number of the answer choice below.

> Citizen opposition to the proposed widening of the intersection at Pine and Oak Streets continues to mount. Dozens of residents turned out to speak at last night's open council meeting. Homeowners living south of Pine Street expressed concern over losing a portion of their neighborhood soccer park. Those west of Oak Street feared an enlarged intersection would invite even more traffic. They objected to the noise and pollution that would result. The mayor and motorists, however, held to their position in favor of the proposal.

_____ **What inference can you make about the current traffic conditions at Pine and Oak Streets?**

(1) Very few citizens care about what might happen to this intersection.
(2) There is a lot of traffic congestion at this intersection.
(3) Traffic at this intersection is heaviest in the mornings.
(4) This intersection doesn't get much traffic.

Skillbuilder 6: Interpreting a Political Cartoon

To illustrate their opinions on a particular subject, cartoonists provide clues using several techniques. These include caricature, in which a person's physical features are exaggerated, and symbols, which represent a concept. Sometimes cartoonists include labels or captions to help readers interpret their message.

Understanding this skill will help you answer questions such as the one shown below. Follow the steps to practice the skill. Then, answer the question on the line provided.

1. Read the question. Then read the caption and any other words printed in the cartoon.
2. Identify the clues: What is happening in the cartoon? What caricatures and symbols are shown in the cartoon? What do these represent?
3. What point is the cartoonist making?
4. Check to see if your conclusion matches any of the answer choices. If not, compare each answer choice to the cartoon to see which is the closest match.
5. Write the number of the best answer on the line below.

_____ **Benjamin Franklin created this image in the 1750s. Which of the following statements best describes Franklin's opinion about the American colonies?**

(1) Some of the colonies are stronger than others, and the weaker ones will die.
(2) If the colonies unite, that will result in a being that possesses the power and force of a snake.
(3) The colonies should remain separate to remain strong.
(4) England is like a snake that has power over the colonies. If the colonies try to unite, England will divide them.

Skillbuilder 7: Making Generalizations

Generalizations are broad statements based on facts. Generalizations can be true (valid) or untrue (invalid). To determine if a generalization is valid, look for evidence that supports it as you read.

Understanding this skill will help you answer questions such as the one shown below. Follow the steps to practice the skill. Then, answer the question on the line provided.

1. Identify the subject matter.
2. Gather related facts and examples from the passage.
3. Identify similarities among these facts.
4. Use these similarities to form a general statement about the subject.
5. Write the number of the best answer on the line below.

> "The reins of government have been so long slackened that I fear the people will not quietly submit to those restraints which are necessary for the peace and security of the community. If we separate from Britain, what code of laws will be established? How shall we be governed so as to retain our liberties? Can any government be free which is administered by general stated laws? Who shall frame these laws? Who will give them force and energy? It is true your resolutions, as a body, have hitherto had the force of laws; but will they continue to have?"
>
> —*Abigail Adams, from a letter to her husband, John*

_____ **Based on information in the letter, which statement is a valid generalization?**

(1) The colonies should adopt the British code of laws.
(2) The Americans should frame new laws.
(3) There are many issues to consider if America separates from Britain.
(4) It would be better if Britain convinced America to adopt its code of laws.

Skillbuilder 8: Reading a Time Line

One way of organizing events is to show them on a time line. A time line is a graphic representation of events arranged in the order in which they happened with dates of their occurrences. Reading a time line helps you view an event in the context and sequence of other events.

Understanding this skill will help you answer questions such as the one shown below. Follow the steps to practice the skill. Then, answer the question on the line provided.

1. Trace the time line from left to right. Note the dates at each end. This tells you the total span of time covered.
2. Notice the shorter segments, or time intervals, marked off along the time line. The segments have a uniform length and might cover days, years, or other blocks of time.
3. Read the title or label above the time line to determine the type of events displayed. There might be a title below the time line, indicating that a different category of events occurred during the same time span.
4. Examine the events contained in the time line. Note which events occurred before or after other events. Observe the length of time separating different events.
5. Read the question. Check each answer choice to see if the events are in the same order as on the time line. If not, list the events in the answers in their correct order.

6. Select the best answer choice. Write the number of the answer choice below.

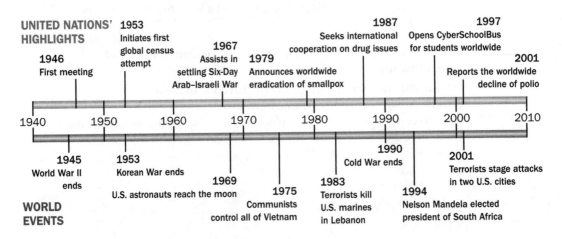

_____ **U.S. astronauts reached the moon**

    (1) before the first meeting of the United Nations

    (2) before the end of the Korean War

    (3) after the United Nations assisted in settling the Six-Day Arab-Israeli War

    (4) after the end of the Cold War

Skillbuilder 9: Distinguishing Fact from Opinion

A **fact** answers a specific question such as *Who? What? Where? When?* or *How many?* Statements of fact can be checked for accuracy and proven. An **opinion** expresses beliefs, feelings, and judgments and cannot be proven to be true or false.

Understanding this skill will help you answer questions such as the one shown below. Follow the steps to practice the skill. Then, answer the question on the line provided.

1. Read the passage and the question. Identify facts by asking what specific information is given and whether it can be proven true or false. Write a fact from the passage and explain how the accuracy of the statement can be checked.

   _____

   _____

2. Identify opinions that express someone's feelings, beliefs, or judgment. Write an opinion from the passage. Explain how you know it is an opinion.

   _____

   _____

3. Reread the question. Check to see whether each answer choice given is a fact or an opinion based on what you know about distinguishing the two types of statements.
4. Write the number of the best answer on the line below.

> President Harding was born in Ohio in 1865. As an adult, he was active in civic and fraternal organizations. He became the 29th president of the United States in 1921. Lasting only two years, his administration suffered many public scandals, including the Teapot Dome scandal in 1922. Harding was the most scandalous president in United States history. After Harding's death in 1923, Vice President Calvin Coolidge took over the White House. Coolidge led the nation for the next several years.

_____ **Which of the following statements from the passage above is an opinion?**

(1) He became the 29th president of the United States in 1921.
(2) Harding was the most scandalous president in United States history.
(3) As an adult, he was active in civic and fraternal organizations.
(4) Coolidge led the nation for the next several years.

Skillbuilder 10: Analyzing News Media

When you read or listen to news media, you need to be aware of a reporter's, publisher's, or station's biases to determine whether the source or report is reliable.

Understanding this skill will help you answer questions such as the one shown below. Follow the steps to practice the skill. Then, answer the question on the line provided.

1. Read the article. Who or what is the source of information in the article? Is this source generally considered to be trustworthy?

   _____

   _____

2. List two points of information from the article.

   _____

   _____

3. Read the question. Write the number of the best answer on the line.

   > People are increasingly spending more time online but not at the cost of family relationships or social activities, says a study to be released Thursday. . . . Jeffrey Cole, director of the UCLA Center for Communication Policy . . . conducted the survey. . . . [C]ontrary to early warnings sounded by some social scientists, the UCLA survey shows overwhelmingly that Internet usage does not take away from normal family activities. Some 97.3 percent of those surveyed said they spend about the same or more time with their family members since being connected to the Internet. . . .

   _____ **Which of the following statements best describes the reliability of this article?**

   (1) It is a poor source because it has to do with the Internet.

   (2) It is a good source because most people will be happy with its findings.

   (3) It is a good source because the survey was carried out and published by a major university.

   (4) It is a poor source because it lacks factual information.

Skillbuilder 11: Making Comparisons

When making comparisons, you examine two or more people, groups, situations, events, or documents. Then you identify similarities and differences.

Understanding this skill will help you answer questions such as the one shown below. Follow the steps to practice the skill. Then, answer the question on the line provided.

1. Decide what items are being compared.
2. Identify the characteristics you will be using to compare them.
3. List how the items being compared are similar.
4. List how the items being compared are different.
5. Write the number of the best answer on the line below.

_____ Compare the powers of the federal government as identified in the Articles of Confederation and the United States Constitution. Which statement is an accurate comparison?

(1) The Constitution specifies additional powers that are not named in the Articles of Confederation.

(2) Under the Articles of Confederation, the government could coin money, impose taxes, and regulate trade; under the Constitution, it could not.

(3) Both documents give the federal government the same powers.

(4) The Articles of Confederation granted the government more power than the Constitution.

Powers of the Federal Government

	Articles of Confederation	United States Constitution
Declare war; make peace	✔	✔
Coin money	✔	✔
Manage foreign affairs	✔	✔
Establish a postal system	✔	✔
Impose taxes		✔
Regulate trade		✔
Organize a court system		✔
Call state militias for service		✔
Protect copyrights		✔
Take other necessary actions to run the federal government		✔

Skillbuilder 12: Analyzing Primary Sources

Primary sources are records of events made by the people who witnessed them. They include letters, diaries, photographs and pictures, news articles, and legal documents.

Understanding this skill will help you answer questions such as the one shown below. Follow the steps to practice the skill. Then, answer the question on the line provided.

1. Identify who created the document, when it was created, what it is about, and why the person created it.

   _____

   _____

   _____

2. Look for information that might be based on the person's opinions rather than facts.
3. Draw conclusions about the reliability of the source.
4. Read the question. Check each answer choice against the passage and against your own conclusions.
5. Select the best answer choice. Write the number of the answer choice on the line below.

> Yesterday afternoon . . . I order'd the troops to be in readiness, . . . but . . . the men were unable to stir on [account] of provision, . . . Soap, vinegar and other articles allowed by Congress we see none of . . . men now in camp [are] unfit for duty because they are bare foot and otherwise naked . . . I much doubt the practicability of holding the army together much longer.
> — *General George Washington, writing in 1777 from Valley Forge*
> *to the Continental Congress*

_____ **Which of the following statements best describes this primary source?**

(1) The purpose of the letter was to convince Congress to declare an end to the war.

(2) George Washington was not a reliable source of information.

(3) Most of the information in the letter is opinion, not fact.

(4) The purpose of the letter was to convince Congress to send needed supplies for the troops.

Skillbuilder 13: Recognizing Bias

A bias is a prejudice. Bias prevents someone from looking at a situation in a reasonable and truthful way. Recognizing bias allows you to identify a particular point of view or prejudice in a passage or account.

Understanding this skill will help you answer questions such as the one shown below. Follow the steps to practice the skill. Then, answer the question on the line provided.

1. Read the passage. Identify the source of information. Ask yourself if the writer is identified with a known group or side of an issue. Who is the author of this passage? How is he identified?

   _____

   _____

2. Look for descriptive and colorful language or emotionally charged words. Use what you already know about the subject of the passage to determine whether any statements are distorted or exaggerated.

3. Read the question. Write the number of the best answer on the line below.

   This excerpt was written around 1820 by Jeremiah Jeter, a Southern slaveholder.

   > I could not free them, for the laws of the State forbade it. Yet even if they had not forbidden it, the slaves in my possession were in no condition to support themselves. It was simple cruelty to free a mother with dependent children. Observation, too, had satisfied me that the free negroes were, in general, in a worse condition than the slaves.

   _____ **Which of the following statements BEST expresses Jeremiah Jeter's point of view?**

   (1) He says that if the State allowed him to free his slaves, he would do it.

   (2) He thinks enslaved African Americans are better off than those who are free.

   (3) He thinks that keeping people enslaved is cruel.

   (4) He supports slavery but is wary of expressing his opinion.

Skillbuilder 14: Reading a Diagram and Flowchart

Diagrams and flowcharts are two ways that information can be presented. A diagram is a chart or drawing that shows where things are located and how they fit together. A flowchart shows the steps in a process or the sequence of events.

Understanding this skill will help you answer questions such as the one shown below. Follow the steps to practice the skill. Then, answer the question on the line provided.

1. Read the title to find out what the diagram or flowchart shows.
2. Read all labels and determine their meanings.
3. If there is a legend, identify the meanings of the symbols and colors used in the diagram or flowchart.
4. Look for numbers indicating a sequence of steps or arrows showing direction of movement.
5. Write the number of the best answer on the line below.

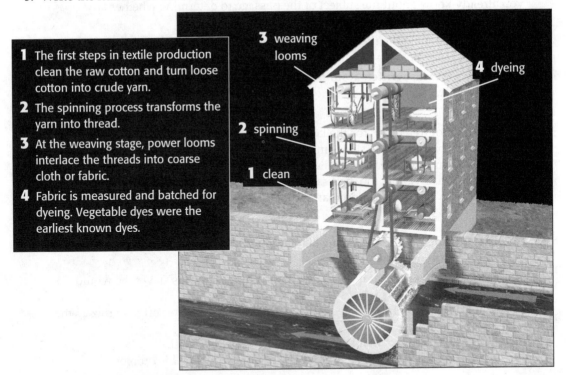

1 The first steps in textile production clean the raw cotton and turn loose cotton into crude yarn.

2 The spinning process transforms the yarn into thread.

3 At the weaving stage, power looms interlace the threads into coarse cloth or fabric.

4 Fabric is measured and batched for dyeing. Vegetable dyes were the earliest known dyes.

3 weaving looms

4 dyeing

2 spinning

1 clean

_____ **Analyze the diagram of the textile mill. Which of the following statements best describes what the diagram shows?**

(1) In 1830, textile mills were powered by water.
(2) Textile mills in 1830 had six rooms.
(3) In 1830, the production of textiles involved four steps.
(4) In 1830, people were not needed in textile mills.

Unit 1—Beginnings to 1500

Overview

Historians, archaeologists, and anthropologists are scientists who study people and events of the past. Historians rely mostly on written records to learn about and interpret history. However, no written records exist for much of the prehistory of humankind—the time before writing was developed. Anthropologists and archaeologists use artifacts, such as tools, pottery, paintings, weapons, and human remains, to determine how ancient peoples lived.

Historians divide history into blocks of time known as periods or eras. They also use geography to understand how location, environment, and physical features shaped the course of past events. Maps are essential tools for historians. Physical maps show the physical features of an area, such as mountains and rivers, while political maps show human-made divisions of countries or regions. Historical maps show how territories change over time.

Scientists are still trying to determine exactly how the first people came to North and South America. Many believe that they crossed over a land bridge that joined Asia and the Americas during the last Ice Age. When the Ice Age ended, the land was submerged under the Bering Strait. Early Americans were nomadic hunters. With the discovery of maize, an early form of corn, a farming culture was born. People were able to settle into more permanent communities.

Several Native American civilizations developed sophisticated cultures before the arrival of Europeans. In Central and South America, groups such as the Maya, Aztec, and Inca built enormous cities and complex road and irrigation systems, and established highly structured forms of government. The Maya produced a 365-day calendar and a system of writing called hieroglyphics, while the Inca developed a system of terrace farming to support their mountainous empire.

East of the Mississippi and south of the Great Lakes lay almost one million miles of woodlands. Most of the peoples who lived in this region were divided into two groups: those who spoke Algonquin languages and those who spoke Iroquois languages. The Algonquin lived mainly in what would become known as New England. The Iroquois lived in what is now northern New York State. The five main groups of Iroquois had similar cultures but often warred with each other until the late 1500s, when they formed an alliance known as the Iroquois League.

Essential Questions

As you prepare for the Intermediate-Level Test in Social Studies, ask yourself these essential questions:

- What tools do historians, archaeologists, and anthropologists use to learn about and interpret history?

- What kinds of different maps do social scientists use and how do maps help them interpret the past?

- How did the Maya, Aztec, and Inca adapt their cultures and civilizations to their surroundings?

- How were the Algonquin and Iroquois peoples similar? How were they different?

Part I: Multiple-Choice Questions

DIRECTIONS: Write the number of the answer that best completes the statement or answers the question.

Causes and Effects of Migration	
Cause	**Effect**
The earth enters a long Ice Age.	Hunters from Asia cross into North America.
Water from the ocean freezes.	People spread into Central America and South America.
Sea levels drop, exposing the Beringia land bridge.	The early Americans create new cultures.

_____ 1. According to the information in the chart, which statement is true?

(1) Early Americans came from Asia because of food shortages.
(2) Early Americans created new cultures because of the Ice Age.
(3) The exposed land bridge allowed hunters from Asia to cross into North America.
(4) Central and South American peoples traveled across the land bridge to explore new lands.

_____ **2.** The early Americans were nomads. Nomads are

(1) people who settle in one place
(2) people who move from place to place
(3) people who fight for land on which they can farm
(4) people who do not believe in hunting

_____ **3.** How did early American nomads hunt for food?

(1) They made spears out of sharpened rocks and poles.
(2) They used bows and arrows.
(3) They grew and harvested all the food they needed.
(4) They built and set traps to catch large animals.

Base your answer to question 4 on the map below and on your knowledge of social studies.

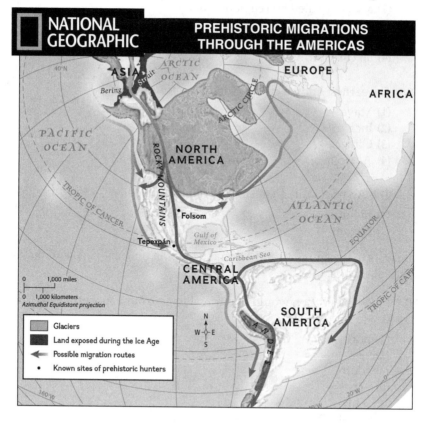

_____ **4.** How was it possible for prehistoric people to cross the Bering Strait?

(1) They crossed the strait in boats.
(2) Early people built a bridge across the strait.
(3) A glacier moved through the area.
(4) A land bridge was exposed that connected Asia to North America.

_____ 5. An early form of corn was

    (1) squash   **(3)** lard

    (2) cilantro   **(4)** maize

_____ 6. Why was farming critical to the development of civilizations across the Americas?

    (1) It allowed people to settle in one place and create unique cultures.

    (2) People did not have to rely on animals for food.

    (3) Crops could be planted anywhere.

    (4) It gave people a greater variety of food.

_____ 7. A civilization is

    (1) a society ruled by religious leaders

    (2) a highly developed society

    (3) a branch of government

    (4) an early form of writing

_____ 8. The earliest known civilization in the Americas is

    (1) Maya

    (2) Inca

    (3) Olmec

    (4) Aztec

_____ 9. The Anasazi built great stone dwellings called

    (1) mounds   **(3)** pueblos

    (2) hogans   **(4)** tepees

Base your answers to questions 10 and 11 on the map on the next page and on your knowledge of social studies.

_____ 10. In what direction would you travel to go from Tenochtitlán to Chichén Itzá?

    (1) north

    (2) east

    (3) south

    (4) west

_____ 11. What was the capital of the Aztec Empire?

    (1) Tenochtitlán

    (2) Cuzco

    (3) Machu Picchu

    (4) Tikal

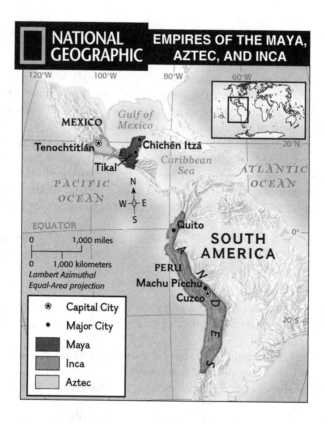

_____ **12.** Which early civilization developed hieroglyphics?

    (1) Maya

    (2) Aztec

    (3) Inca

    (4) Mound Builders

_____ **13.** What effect did the mountainous terrain of the Incan Empire have on the development of farming?

    (1) They had to trade for food with other civilizations.

    (2) The Inca could only grow certain crops on their land.

    (3) They cut terraces in the mountains to create land to plant crops.

    (4) The Inca depended on hunting for their food.

_____ **14.** How did the appearance of wild horses change the lifestyle of Native Americans on the Great Plains?

    (1) The Native Americans were unable to tame the wild horses.

    (2) The wild horses made life harder for the Native Americans.

    (3) The Native Americans used the wild horses as another food source.

    (4) The Native Americans used the horses to aid in hunting and warfare.

Base your answers to questions 15 and 16 on the following passage and on your knowledge of social studies.

> "We Lakota people have a prophecy about a white buffalo calf. How that prophecy originated was that we have a sacred bundle, a sacred pipe, that was brought to us about 2,000 years ago. . . . They say a cloud came down from the sky, and off of the cloud stepped the white buffalo calf. As it rolled onto the earth, the calf stood up and became this beautiful young woman who was carrying the sacred bundle in her hand. . . . And she instructed our people that as long as we performed these ceremonies we would always remain caretakers and guardians of sacred land. She told us that as long as we took care of it and respected it that our people would never die and would always live."
>
> *—Joseph Chasing Horse of the Lakota People*
> *tells of the White Buffalo Calf Woman*

_____ 15. Which of the following statements BEST describes this primary source?
   (1) The speaker is telling a story about the origins of his people.
   (2) The purpose of this story is to demonstrate the superiority of the Lakota.
   (3) The Lakota believe that as long as they respect and care for their land, their people will live forever.
   (4) The story is not a reliable source of information about the Lakota.

_____ 16. What inference can you make about the Lakota after reading this passage?
   (1) They have lived on their lands for thousands of years.
   (2) They were a nomadic people.
   (3) They have many ceremonies to celebrate the White Buffalo Calf Woman.
   (4) The calf is a sacred animal to the Lakota.

Base your answer to question 17 on the chart below and on your knowledge of social studies.

Culture	Region	Shelter
Algonquin	New England	longhouses
Iroquois	Upper New York State	longhouses
Anasazi	Southwestern United States	pueblos
Inuit	Northernmost United States	igloos

_____ 17. What would be the most appropriate title for the chart?

(1) Early European Peoples
(2) Inuit Shelters
(3) South American Civilizations
(4) Early Peoples of the United States

_____ 18. In Iroquois culture, who chose the representatives to the Iroquois League council?

(1) tribe elders   (3) women of the tribe
(2) tribal chiefs   (4) Representatives were elected.

_____ 19. How is prehistory different from history?

(1) Prehistory was written before history.
(2) There are no written records of prehistory.
(3) Historians don't know anything about prehistory.
(4) Our knowledge of prehistory is based on written documents.

_____ 20. Which of the following is an example of a primary source?

(1) biography
(2) letter
(3) textbook
(4) encyclopedia

_____ 21. Scientists who search for artifacts—weapons, tools, fossils, etc.—are called

(1) archaeologists
(2) anthropologists
(3) historians
(4) paleontologists

Part II: Constructed-Response Questions

DIRECTIONS: *Analyze the passage below. Then answer the questions based on the passage and on your knowledge of social studies.*

> True farming began to emerge in the eastern woodlands [of North America] once hardier strains of maize and beans appeared after A.D. 700. The resulting growth in food production stimulated the rise of North America's first towns, in the Mississippi basin, by the twelfth century. These centered around large earthwork temple mounds. The Mississippian cultures shared a common religion known as the Southern Cult and were hierarchical. Large Mississippian towns, such as Cahokia, were the centers of powerful chiefdoms.

1. What did the typical Mississippian diet consist of?

   _____

   _____

   _____

2. Was Cahokia the only large Mississipian town? Explain your answer.

   _____

   _____

   _____

3. Approximately how long after the farming of maize and beans began did it take for the first towns to emerge?

   _____

   _____

   _____

DIRECTIONS: *Study the maps below. Then answer the questions based on the maps and on your knowledge of social studies.*

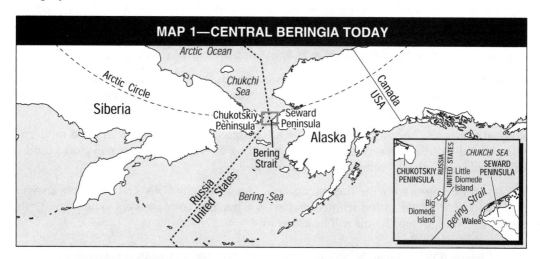

MAP 1—CENTRAL BERINGIA TODAY

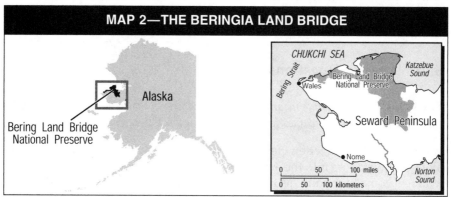

MAP 2—THE BERINGIA LAND BRIDGE

4. What countries are included in the geographic region of Beringia today?

_____

_____

5. Which bodies of water bordered the Beringia Land Bridge?

_____

_____

6. How do you think sea life such as whales were affected while the land bridge connected Asia and North America?

_____

_____

Part III: Document-Based Questions

This exercise is designed to test your ability to work with historical documents. It is similar to the document-based questions that you will see on the Intermediate-Level Test in Social Studies. While you are asked to analyze three historical documents, the exercise on the Intermediate-Level Test in Social Studies may include up to nine documents.

Some of the documents have been edited for the purposes of the question. As you analyze the documents, take into account the source of each document and any point of view that may be presented in the document.

Historical Context: The spirit of exploration has inspired people from ancient and modern civilizations alike. The effects of exploration, including interactions between explorers and native peoples, have been both positive and negative.

Task: Use information from the documents and your knowledge of social studies to answer the questions that follow each document in Part A. Then use your answers to help you write the essay in Part B, in which you will be asked to:

> Analyze the interactions between early explorers and native peoples. Discuss both positive and negative aspects of those interactions and how each group viewed the other.

Part A: Short-Answer Questions

DIRECTIONS: *Analyze the documents and answer the questions that follow each document in the space provided. Your answers to the questions will help you write the essay.*

Document 1 In the following letter, Hernán Cortés described Montezuma's reception of him and his fellow conquistadors into the Aztec capital of Tenochtitlán in 1519. Believing Cortés to be a god who had come to reclaim his kingdom, Montezuma (also known as Moctezuma) showered the Spaniards with gifts and generously offered them complete access to the city, including his own palace. Montezuma discovered too late the visitors' true identities, as the Spaniards quickly overpowered the king and seized control of the city and all its riches.

. . . He sat on another throne which they had placed there next to the one on which I was sitting, and addressed me in the following way:

"For a long time we have known from the writings of our ancestors that neither I [Moctezuma], nor any of those who dwell in this land, are natives of it, but foreigners who came from very distant parts; and likewise we knew that a chieftain, of whom they were all vassals, brought our people to this region. And he who returned to his native land and after many years came again, by which time all those who had remained were married to native women and had built villages and raised children. . . . "

Then he raised his clothes and showed me his body, saying, and he grasped his arms and trunk with his hands, "See that I am of flesh and blood like you and all other men, and I am mortal and substantial. See how they have lied to you? It is true that I have some pieces of gold left to me by my ancestors; anything I might have shall be given to you whenever you ask. Now I shall go to other houses where I live, but here you shall be provided with all that you and your people required, and you shall receive no hurt, for you are in your own land and your own house."

1.*a* How does Montezuma treat Cortés and his followers?

_____

_____

b What does Montezuma offer the Spaniards? Why?

_____

_____

c What did Cortés and his men feel about Montezuma?

_____

_____

Document 2 The Native Americans left few written records of the arrival of the Spanish conqueror Hernán Cortés in Tenochtitlán (today's Mexico City) in 1519. From them, however, Miguel León Portillo, a Mexican anthropologist, constructed an eyewitness account of how Cortés treated the Native Americans and seized Montezuma (also known as Montecuhzoma) before going on to destroy the city and to take over much of what is present-day Mexico.

> When the Spanish entered the Royal House, they placed Montecuhzoma under guard and kept him under their vigilance. They also placed a guard over Itzcuauhtzin, but the other lords were permitted to depart.
>
> Then the Spaniards fired one of their cannons, and this caused great confusion in the city. The people scattered in every direction; they fled without rhyme or reason; they ran off as if they were being pursued. It was as if they had eaten the mushrooms that confuse the mind, or had seen some dreadful apparition. They were all overcome by terror, as if their hearts had fainted. And when night fell, the panic spread throughout the city and their fears would not let them sleep.
>
> When the Spanish were installed in the palace, they asked Montecuhzoma about the city's resources and reserves and about the warriors' ensigns and shields. They questioned him closely and then demanded gold.

2._a_ How did the Spanish cause fear and confusion among the Aztec?

_____

_____

_b_ How did Montezuma's messengers describe Cortés and his troops?

_____

_____

_c_ How did Cortés and his troops treat the Native Americans?

_____

_____

Document 3 Francisco Vásquez de Coronado was a Spanish governor in western Mexico when he heard tales about seven cities of gold to the north and set out in search of them in 1540. What he found instead were some poor Zuni villages in what is today New Mexico. Determined to locate gold, Coronado headed east in search of the reputedly rich land of Quivira and may have traveled as far as present-day Kansas. He later sent an account of his explorations to Charles I of Spain.

I have treated the natives of this province, and all the others whom I found wherever I went, as well as was possible, agreeably to what Your Majesty had commanded, and they have received no harm in any way from me or from those who went in my company. . . . The guides who had brought me had given me an account of other provinces beyond this. And what I am sure of is that there is not any gold nor any other metal in all that country, and the other things of which they had told me are nothing but little villages, and in many of these they do not plant anything and do not have any houses except of skins and sticks, and they wander around with the cows; so that the account they gave me was false, because they wanted to persuade me to go there with the whole force, believing that as the way was through such uninhabited deserts, and from the lack of water, they would get us where we and our horses would die of hunger. And the guides confessed this, and said they had done it by the advice and orders of the natives of these provinces. At this, after having heard the account of what was beyond, which I have given above, I returned to these provinces to provide for the force I had sent back here . . .

3._a_ Why did Coronado write this account?

_b_ How did the native people that Coronado encountered live?

_c_ How did the native people Coronado encountered feel about him? How do you know?

Part B: Essay

DIRECTIONS: _Write a well-organized essay that includes an introduction, several paragraphs, and a conclusion. Use evidence from the three documents in the body of the essay. Support your response with relevant facts, examples, and details. Include additional outside information._

Analyze the interactions between early explorers and native peoples. Discuss both positive and negative aspects of those interactions and how each group viewed the other.

Unit 2—European Exploration and Colonization, *1500–1754*

Overview

Europeans were dependent on Arab traders for Asian goods such as silks, perfumes, and especially spices. These merchants charged high prices. Early European explorers were searching for new trade routes so that they did not have to depend on these merchants.

Advances in technology and more accurate maps, which came from China and the Middle East, paved the way for European exploration. The maps available to early explorers did not include the Americas, however, and they also underestimated the size of the oceans. In setting sail across the Atlantic Ocean, Christopher Columbus thought when he reached land that he had arrived at the East Indies, islands off the coast of Asia. He had actually landed in the Caribbean Islands. He called the native people he encountered *Indians.*

Europeans were looking for new routes to Asia so they could profit from trade. Sailing under the Spanish flag, Italian Christopher Columbus attempted to reach Asia by sailing west instead of east, as others before him had done. He first landed on a small island in the Bahamas.

Later, Spain sent many expeditions to search for gold and silver and to conquer native peoples in the Americas. With weapons such as guns and cannons, the conquistadors easily succeeded in defeating Native Americans in Peru and Mexico. The native people were also devastated by European diseases, to which they had no immunity.

In North America, the British, French, and Dutch all established colonies. People came to the "New World" in search of wealth and religious freedom. Farming was important to all the colonies. Economies in the South depended on crops such as tobacco and rice. Northern colonies developed industries such as shipbuilding. Differences in the types of farming and economic development were due to the varying climate and geography in each region.

As the colonies grew and prospered, the need for cheap labor increased. Slavery, which had existed in the colonies since their earliest days, grew at an extremely rapid pace. In exchange for goods from Europe and the Americas, West African kingdoms would sell prisoners of war to traders bound for America.

Early governments were largely influenced by English traditions. Limited and representative governments took hold in most of the colonies. White men who owned property were allowed to vote; women and enslaved people were not. People in the colonies were largely literate and many communities established schools for children to attend.

Essential Questions

As you prepare for the Intermediate-Level Test in Social Studies, ask yourself these essential questions:

- What were the major causes and effects of European exploration?

- How was Native American culture impacted by the arrival of the Europeans?

- How did settlers adapt to the new environments?

- How did colonial economies develop and how did they differ from each other?

- What were the causes of the differences in the colonies?

Part I: Multiple-Choice Questions

DIRECTIONS: *Write the number of the answer that best completes the statement or answers the question.*

Base your answers to questions 1 and 2 on the following passage and on your knowledge of social studies.

> "October 11: The crew of the *Pinta* spotted some . . . reed and some other plants; they also saw what looked like a small board or plank. A stick was recovered that looks manmade, perhaps carved with an iron tool . . . but even these few [things] made the crew breathe easier; in fact the men have even become cheerful.
>
> October 12: The islanders came to the ships' boats, swimming and bringing us parrots and balls of cotton thread . . . which they exchanged for . . . glass beads and hawk bells . . . they took and gave of what they had very willingly, but it seemed to me that they were poor in every way. They bore no weapons, nor were they acquainted with them, because when I showed them swords they seized them by the edge and so cut themselves from ignorance."
> —*from the diaries of Christopher Columbus, 1492*

_____ 1. Why were members of Columbus's crew cheerful when they spied the objects at sea?

(1) They needed supplies.
(2) They knew that they were close to land.
(3) They thought they were close to home.
(4) The *Pinta* needed to be repaired with the wood they found.

_____ 2. How did Columbus react to the native people he encountered?

(1) He thought he could learn from them.
(2) He was suspicious of them.
(3) He believed they were not as smart as the Europeans.
(4) He was very happy to see them.

_____ 3. I. _____

    A. Artistic creativity: Michelangelo's *David* and Leonardo da Vinci's *Mona Lisa*

    B. Intellectual creativity: Dante's *Divine Comedy*

    C. Printing press

    D. Medici family

Which heading best completes the partial outline above?

    (1) Reformation

    (2) Renaissance

    (3) Restoration

    (4) Recreation

_____ 4. What did European missionaries try to accomplish in the New World?

    (1) establish new trade routes

    (2) enslave African Americans

    (3) found colonies to boost trade

    (4) convert native peoples to Christianity

_____ 5. Which two countries turned to the pope in 1493 to settle territorial disputes?

    (1) Spain and Portugal

    (2) England and France

    (3) England and Spain

    (4) France and Spain

Base your answers to questions 6 and 7 on the time line below and on your knowledge of social studies.

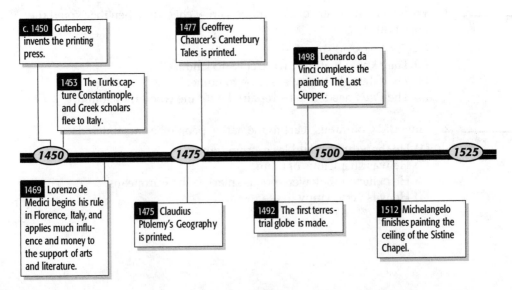

c. 1450 Gutenberg invents the printing press.

1477 Geoffrey Chaucer's Canterbury Tales is printed.

1498 Leonardo da Vinci completes the painting The Last Supper.

1453 The Turks capture Constantinople, and Greek scholars flee to Italy.

1450   1475   1500   1525

1469 Lorenzo de Medici begins his rule in Florence, Italy, and applies much influence and money to the support of arts and literature.

1475 Claudius Ptolemy's Geography is printed.

1492 The first terrestrial globe is made.

1512 Michelangelo finishes painting the ceiling of the Sistine Chapel.

_____ **6.** When did Gutenberg invent the printing press?

    (1) 1500   **(3)** 1450

    (2) 1525   **(4)** 1492

_____ **7.** What span of time does the time line represent?

    (1) 100 years   **(3)** 25 years

    (2) 50 years   **(4)** 75 years

_____ **8.** Which was an impact of the printing press?

    (1) New ideas spread much more quickly.

    (2) Colonists left for America to search for religious freedom.

    (3) Explorers had better data to use for exploration.

    (4) Strong monarchs came to power in France, Spain, England, and Portugal.

Base your answers to questions 9 and 10 on the time line below and on your knowledge of social studies.

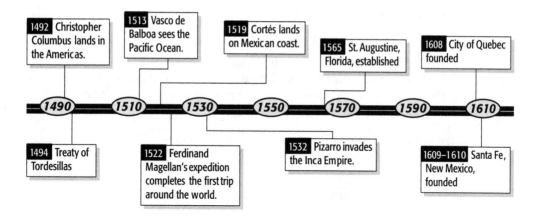

_____ **9.** How many years after Cortés landed on the coast of Mexico did Pizarro invade the Inca Empire?

    (1) 15 years

    (2) 22 years

    (3) 20 years

    (4) 13 years

_____ **10.** Which city was established first?

    (1) Quebec

    (2) St. Augustine

    (3) Santa Fe

    (4) Las Vegas

_____ **11.** Why did Spain finance Columbus's voyage?

(1) so that Columbus could find the islands now called the Bahamas
(2) so that Columbus could find new land for Portugal
(3) so that Columbus could find America
(4) so that Columbus could find a trade route to Asia

_____ **12.** Which was a reason that the Spanish were able to defeat Native American empires?

(1) the discovery of the fountain of youth by Ponce de Leon
(2) the Spanish had bigger, faster ships
(3) the arrival of European diseases, such as smallpox, caused epidemics
(4) the Spanish brought gifts for native leaders

_____ **13.** Las Casas, a Spanish priest, tried to protect

(1) the Native Americans who were turned into slaves
(2) the cattle and horses brought to the Pueblo people
(3) the *peninsulares*—the upper-class people
(4) the Spanish government

_____ **14.** Which statement best describes European life and religion in the 1500s?

(1) Catholics and Protestants lived together peacefully.
(2) Many European countries broke away from the Catholic Church.
(3) European countries remained bound together by a common church.
(4) Freedom of religion was encouraged.

_____ **15.**

Exploration of North America	
Causes	**Effects**
Protestant Reformation	Protestants sought religious freedom in North America
Search for Northwest Passage	
Early trading activities	French, Dutch, and English establish fur-trading posts

Which of the following would best complete the chart above?

(1) Exploration of present-day Canada
(2) Discovery of a more direct water route to Asia
(3) Discovery of the St. Lawrence River
(4) Exploration west of the Mississippi

Base your answers to questions 16 and 17 on the chart and on your knowledge of social studies.

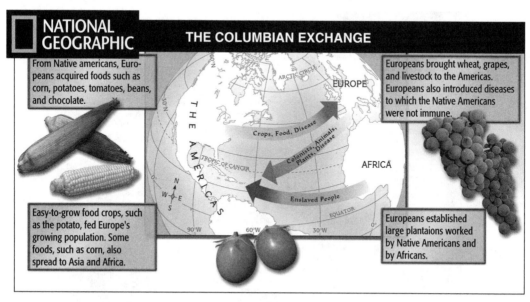

NATIONAL GEOGRAPHIC   **THE COLUMBIAN EXCHANGE**

From Native americans, Europeans acquired foods such as corn, potatoes, tomatoes, beans, and chocolate.

Europeans brought wheat, grapes, and livestock to the Americas. Europeans also introduced diseases to which the Native Americans were not immune.

Easy-to-grow food crops, such as the potato, fed Europe's growing population. Some foods, such as corn, also spread to Asia and Africa.

Europeans established large plantaions worked by Native Americans and by Africans.

Crops, Food, Disease

Colonists, Animals, Plants, Disease

Enslaved People

EUROPE

AFRICA

_____ **16.** Who benefited most from the Columbian Exchange?

(1) Europeans
(2) Africans
(3) Native Americans
(4) colonial settlers

_____ **17.** Which item came from Europe to America?

(1) potatoes
(2) beans
(3) grapes
(4) chocolate

_____ **18.** Why did the Virginia Company want to establish a colony in North America?

(1) to name it Jamestown in honor of their king
(2) to search for gold and set up trade in fish and furs
(3) to learn about farming from the Native Americans
(4) to bring an end to the war with Spain

_____ **19.** Why did settlers choose to build Jamestown on a peninsula?

(1) It made it easier for new arrivals to find the site.
(2) The land was ideal for farming.
(3) It protected the settlers from harsh weather.
(4) It allowed the settlers to easily defend themselves against attack.

Base your answers to questions 20 and 21 on the map below and on your knowledge of social studies.

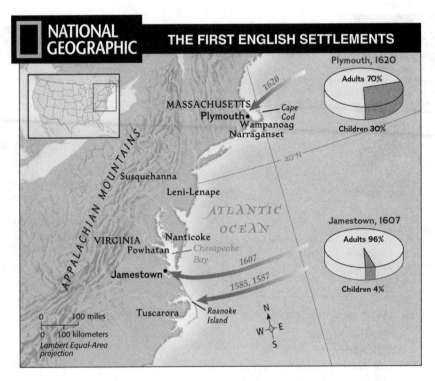

THE FIRST ENGLISH SETTLEMENTS

_____ 20. According to the map, which statement is true?

(1) Plymouth was surrounded by more Native American groups than Jamestown.
(2) Plymouth was founded before Jamestown.
(3) Plymouth had more people than Jamestown.
(4) Plymouth was farther north than Jamestown.

_____ 21. Which statement about Jamestown and Plymouth is supported by the circle graphs?

(1) Jamestown had more children than Plymouth.
(2) Jamestown was larger than Plymouth.
(3) Plymouth had a smaller percentage of children than Jamestown.
(4) Jamestown had a greater percentage of adults than Plymouth.

_____ 22. What economic activity helped save the Jamestown settlement?

(1) growing tobacco
(2) selling land
(3) raising cattle
(4) growing corn

_____ **23.** Why was the House of Burgesses important?

(1) It allowed Virginia settlers to participate in making the laws.
(2) It sent 90 women to Jamestown to encourage marriage and children.
(3) It organized the transfer of Africans to help work in the fields.
(4) It established private ownership of land for the colonists.

_____ **24.** For what reason, other than lack of work, did the Separatists leave the Netherlands?

(1) They worried that their children were losing their English way of life.
(2) They wanted religious freedom found only in the Virginia colony.
(3) The Mayflower Compact required that they leave.
(4) They wished to rejoin the Puritans in England.

Base your answers to questions 25 and 26 on the bar graph and on your knowledge of social studies.

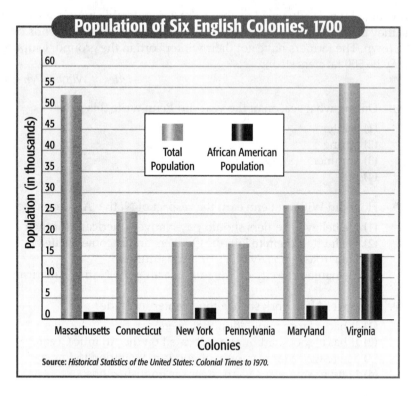

_____ **25.** Which colony had the greatest population of African Americans in 1700?

(1) New York
(2) Maryland
(3) Virginia
(4) Massachusetts

_____ 26. Why did the Southern Colonies have a greater concentration of African Americans?

(1) They were the first to bring slaves to the Americas.
(2) African Americans had greater freedoms there.
(3) The Southern Colonies needed slaves to work on farms and in rice paddies.
(4) Many African Americans settled there because it was similar to their native land.

_____ 27. Which colony was founded for the Quakers?

(1) Rhode Island
(2) Maryland
(3) Pennsylvania
(4) New Jersey

"Our capital town is advanced to about 150 very tolerable houses for wooden ones; they are chiefly on both the navigable rivers that bound the ends or sides of the town. The farmers have got their winter corn in the ground. I suppose we may be 500 farmers strong . . . "

—*letter of William Penn, 1683*

_____ 28. During what season of the year did Penn write this letter?

(1) winter
(2) spring
(3) summer
(4) fall

_____ 29. How did William Penn earn the respect of Native Americans?

(1) He believed settlers should pay Native Americans for their land.
(2) He invited them to join the Quakers and become pacifists.
(3) He wrote Pennsylvania's first constitution.
(4) He named the city of Philadelphia after the Native Americans.

_____ 30. Why was New York such a good center for trade?

(1) It had a large population that needed goods.
(2) It has a good harbor and is located on the Atlantic Ocean.
(3) There was a large supply of goods to be traded to England.
(4) Native Americans were eager for English goods.

31. How did the economic activities of the French differ from those of the English in North America?

   (1) The French settled in present-day Canada, while the English were only interested in Southern colonies.
   (2) The English traded only in gold and silver, while the French traded only in furs.
   (3) The French were interested in trapping and trading, while the English were also interested in building large, permanent settlements.
   (4) The economic activities of the French and English did not differ.

32. Causes of European exploration

      A. gain safer trade routes to East Asia
      B. pursuit of new ideas and goals
      C. _____

Which of the following would best complete the list above?

   (1) knowledge of new cultures
   (2) expansion of trade with newly discovered territories
   (3) desire for religious freedom
   (4) New technologies made exploration possible.

Base your answers to questions 33 and 34 on the map below and on your knowledge of social studies.

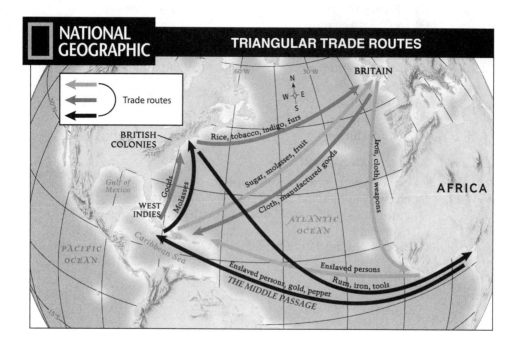

_____ 33. What did the colonies export to Africa?

    (1) rum, iron, and tools
    (2) enslaved persons
    (3) sugar, molasses, and fruit
    (4) cloth and manufactured goods

_____ 34. Which country were most enslaved people sent to?

    (1) British America and the United States
    (2) West Indies
    (3) Brazil
    (4) Spanish South America

Base your answer to question 35 on the quotation below and on your knowledge of social studies.

> "I was soon put down under the decks. . . . The closeness of the place, and the heat of the climate, added to the number in the ship, which was so crowded that each had scarcely room to turn himself, almost suffocated us. . . . The shrieks of the women, and the groans of the dying, rendered [made] the whole a scene of horror."

_____ 35. Who do you think is speaking in the passage above?

    (1) a Spanish conquistador
    (2) a French trapper
    (3) an English colonist
    (4) an enslaved person

_____ 36. What was the main economic activity in all the colonies?

    (1) fishing
    (2) farming
    (3) shipbuilding
    (4) manufacturing

_____ 37. What were cash crops?

    (1) crops that grew well in the Americas
    (2) crops from England that were sold in America
    (3) crops that could be sold easily in markets in the colonies and overseas
    (4) crops from the Southern Colonies

Base your answer to question 38 on the passage below and on your knowledge of social studies.

> Good Children must,
> Fear God all Day,
> Parents Obey
> No false thing say,
> By no Sin stray,
> In doing Good.
> Love Christ alway,
> In Secret Pray,
> Mind little Play,
> Make no delay

_____ **38.** According to the passage, what was the most important thing good children should do?

(1) obey their parents

(2) do their work as quickly as possible

(3) fear God

(4) not tell lies

Part II: Constructed-Response Questions

DIRECTIONS: *Read the paragraph below. Then answer the questions based on the reading and on your knowledge of social studies.*

> . . . We know our lands are now become more valuable; the white people think we do not know their value; but we are sensible that the land is everlasting, and the few goods we receive for it are soon worn out and gone. . . . Your people daily settle on these lands, and spoil our hunting. We must insist upon your removing them. . . . We . . . desire you will inform the people who are seated on our lands, that that country belongs to us, in right of conquest; we having bought it with our blood, and taken it from our enemies in fair war; and we expect, as owner of that land, to receive such a consideration for it as the land is worth.
>
> —*1742 speech by Iroquois Chief Cannassatego*

1. What does Chief Cannassatego say about the value of land as compared to the value of goods?

_____

_____

_____

2. According to Chief Cannassatego, why do the lands in question belong to the Iroquois?

_____

_____

_____

3. What other differences did Native Americans and Europeans have over land ownership?

_____

_____

_____

DIRECTIONS: *Read the paragraph below. Then answer the questions based on the reading and on your knowledge of social studies.*

> . . . the blacks who brought me on board went off, and left me abandoned to despair. I now saw myself deprived of all chance of returning to my native country, or even the least glimpse of hope of gaining the shore, which I now considered friendly: and I even wished for my former slavery in preference to my present situation, which was filled with horrors of every kind, still heightened by my ignorance of what I was to undergo. I was not long suffered to indulge my grief; I was soon put down under the decks, and there I received such a salutation in my nostrils as I had never experienced in my life; so that with the loathsomeness of the stench, and crying together, I became so sick and low that I was not able to eat, nor had I the least desire to taste any thing. I now wished for the last friend, Death, to relieve me. . . .
> —*from the autobiography of Olaudah Equiano (c. 1750–1797)*

1. What does Olaudah Equiano say about the conditions on the ship?

_____

_____

2. How does Olaudah's current situation compare to life before he was brought on the ship?

_____

_____

_____

3. What does Olaudah mean when he says, "I now wished for the last friend, Death, to relieve me"?

_____

_____

_____

Part III: Document-Based Questions

This exercise is designed to test your ability to work with historical documents. It is similar to the document-based questions that you will see on the Intermediate-Level Test in Social Studies. While you are asked to analyze three historical documents, the exercise on the Intermediate-Level Test in Social Studies may include up to nine documents.

Some of the documents have been edited for the purposes of the question. As you analyze the documents, take into account the source of each document and any point of view that may be presented in the document.

Historical Context: The American colonies mixed people from different cultures. Life in the colonies required cooperation, and people often overlooked their cultural differences in order to survive. However, these differences sometimes caused problems.

Task: Use information from the documents and your knowledge of social studies to answer the questions that follow each document in Part A. Then use your answers to help you write the essay in Part B, in which you will be asked to:

> Analyze the positive and negative effects of Europeans establishing American colonies and interacting with Native Americans.

Part A: Short-Answer Questions

DIRECTIONS: Analyze the documents and answer the questions that follow each document in the space provided. Your answers to the questions will help you write the essay.

Document 1 J. Hector St. John Crevecoeur of France, writing about American colonists

> . . . What then is the American, this new man? He is either a European, or the descendant of a European, hence that strange mixture of blood, which you will find in no other country. I could point out to you a family whose grandfather was an Englishman, whose wife was Dutch, and whose son married a French woman, and whose present four sons have now four wives of different nations. . . . There is room for everybody in America; has he particular talent, or industry? He exerts it in order to produce a livelihood, and it succeeds. . . .

1.*a* Why does Crevecoeur refer to Americans as "new"?

_____

_____

_____

  b What does Crevecoeur mean when he writes, "There is room for everybody in America"?

_____

_____

_____

  c Who does Crevecoeur consider a European?

_____

_____

_____

Document 2 Ottowa leader Pontiac addresses an assembly of Potawatomie, Huron, and Ottawa peoples in this 1763 speech

> . . . When I go to see the English commander and say to him that some of our comrades are dead, instead of bewailing their death, as our French brothers do, he laughs at me and you. If I ask for anything for our sick, he refuses with the reply that he has no use for us. From all this you can well see that they are seeking our ruin. Therefore, my brothers, we must all swear their destruction and wait no longer. Nothing prevents us: They are few in numbers, and we can accomplish it. . . .

2.*a* What grievances does Pontiac have against the British colonists?

_____

_____

_____

  b What action does Pontiac suggest that he and the group he had gathered take?

_____

_____

_____

Document 3 Englishman Andrew Burnaby, from his book about his experience living in the colonies for two years

> . . . From what has been said of this colony, it will not be difficult to form an idea of the character of its inhabitants. The climate and external appearance of the country conspire to make them indolent [lazy], easy, and good-natured; extremely fond of society, and much given to convivial [sociable] pleasures. In consequence of this, they seldom show any spirit of enterprise, or expose themselves willingly to fatigue. Their authority over their slaves renders them vain and imperious, and intire [entire] strangers to that elegance of sentiment, which is so peculiarly characteristic of refined and polished nations. Their ignorance of mankind and of learning, exposes them to many errors and prejudices, especially in regard to Indians and Negroes, whom they scarcely consider as of the human species; so that it is almost impossible, in cases of violence, or even murder, committed on those unhappy people by any of the planters, to have the delinquents brought to justice.

3.*a* How does Burnaby feel about the character of the colonists?

_____

_____

_____

b Why did the colonists have errors in prejudices in regard to "Indians and Negroes"?

_____

_____

_____

Part B: Essay

DIRECTIONS: *Write a well-organized essay that includes an introduction, several paragraphs, and a conclusion. Use evidence from the three documents in the body of the essay. Support your response with relevant facts, examples, and details. Include additional outside information.*

> Analyze the positive and negative effects of Europeans establishing American colonies and interacting with Native Americans.

Unit 3—Road to Independence, *1754–1783*

Overview

As British colonies expanded, they pushed up against French territory. A series of skirmishes increased tensions between the two powers. Native Americans largely sided with the French, who generally did not take over Native American land. However, the Iroquois Confederation sided with the British. After the British victory at Quebec, the French signed the Treaty of Paris in 1763, which gave Britain most of the lands east of the Mississippi.

A spirit of independence became evident early in the history of the American people. Far from the established rules and restrictions they had faced in the countries from which they came, the new settlers began to make their own laws and develop their own ways of doing things. Colonists became alarmed at new regulations and taxes designed to increase British revenues. Tensions increased when violence erupted in 1770 in the Boston Massacre.

The first shots of the American Revolution were fired on April 19, 1775, in Lexington, Massachusetts. Battles were fought in every region of the colonies. By July 1776, the colonists were ready to declare their independence. The British surrendered in 1781. When a peace treaty was signed in 1783, the United States was finally recognized as a free and independent nation.

Essential Questions

As you prepare for the Intermediate-Level Test in Social Studies, ask yourself these questions:

- What were the causes of the French and Indian War?
- Why did the American colonists object to new British laws?
- How did the British government try to maintain its control over the colonies?
- What event began the American Revolution?
- Why did the colonists draft the Declaration of Independence?

Part I: Multiple-Choice Questions

DIRECTIONS: *Write the number of the answer that best completes the statement or answers the question.*

_____ 1. Which of the following restricted colonists' trade and limited ship use?

(1) English Bill of Rights
(2) Magna Carta
(3) mercantilism
(4) Navigation Acts

_____ 2. Under the system of mercantilism, what did the colonies provide to England?

(1) manufactured goods
(2) crops
(3) raw materials
(4) ships

_____ 3. What was the purpose of the Navigation Acts?

(1) to direct the flow of goods between England and the colonies
(2) to establish trade routes between England and the colonies
(3) to create new maps chartering the colonies
(4) to establish directions for further exploration of North America

_____ 4. Which of the following was an effect of the Great Awakening?

(1) Awareness of the importance of religion in people's lives grew.
(2) A religious revival swept through America in the mid-1700s.
(3) New governments were established in the colonies.
(4) Belief that all people are equal before God grew.

_____ 5. Why did Alexander Hamilton defend John Peter Zenger and free speech?

(1) He believed that free speech was a basic right of English people.
(2) He agreed with Zenger's criticism of the governor of New York.
(3) He believed that only members of the press should be able to express an opinion about government.
(4) He thought that Zenger's article was true.

_____ 6. Why did Benjamin Franklin's Albany Plan of Union fail?

(1) The colonies wanted to collect taxes, raise troops, and regulate trade.
(2) Of the 11 colonies, only four approved the plan.
(3) The Iroquois agreed to fight against the French.
(4) The colonies were unwilling to give up some power to form a union.

_____ 7. One reason the French felt threatened by the British was because

(1) Britain returned Louisbourg to France

(2) the British were skilled fur traders

(3) the British wanted land in the Ohio River Valley

(4) the French built forts close to the British colonies

_____ 8. Why were the Native Americans more likely to help the French than the British?

(1) The French offered Native Americans lands in France for their help.

(2) The British did not want to take land from the Native Americans.

(3) The French did not take land away from Native Americans.

(4) The French promised to leave if the Native Americans helped them defeat the British.

_____ 9. Why was General Braddock's army defeated in the French and Indian War?

(1) His army's style of marching and bright uniforms were weaknesses.

(2) Braddock listened to and followed Washington's poor advice.

(3) Braddock was not provided with enough British soldiers.

(4) Braddock did not have the support of the British.

_____ 10. What lands did Spain receive under the Treaty of Paris in 1763?

(1) lands east of the Mississippi

(2) Florida

(3) Louisiana Territory and the Port of New Orleans

(4) Spain did not receive any lands.

_____ 11. British Parliament passed a law that placed a tax on almost all printed material in the colonies. What was this law called?

(1) Sugar Act

(2) Writs of Assistance Act

(3) Townshend Acts

(4) Stamp Act

_____ 12. Which term is used to describe the refusal to buy a particular good?

(1) effigy   (3) smuggle

(2) boycott   (4) revenue

_____ 13. Which of the following was a result of Britain passing the Stamp Act?

(1) Colonists boycotted British goods.

(2) Britain repealed the Stamp Act.

(3) Britain needed the money the Stamp Act provided.

(4) Britain passed the Townshend Acts.

Base your answer to question 14 on the excerpt below and on your knowledge of social studies.

> "He who goes voluntarily to America, cannot complain of losing what he leaves in Europe. By his own choice he has left a country, where he had a vote and little property, for another, where he has great property, but no vote."
>
> —*Samuel Johnson*

_____ **14.** Which of the following best describes how the writer feels about the colonists?

    (1) They have left England for a better life.
    (2) They deserve the right to vote.
    (3) They reap the benefits of living in America and shouldn't complain about being taxed.
    (4) They should fight for their independence.

_____ **15.** Which event contributed to the repeal of the Townshend Acts?

    (1) Boston Tea Party
    (2) Boston Massacre
    (3) Daughters of Liberty
    (4) French and Indian War

Base your answers to questions 16 and 17 on the passage below and on your knowledge of social studies.

> The tea was conveyed to the daughter's door,
> All down by the ocean's side,
> And the bouncing girl poured out every pour:
> In the dark and boiling tide;
> And then she called out to the island queen,
> "Oh mother, dear mother," quoth she,
> "Your tea you may have when 'tis steeped quote
> But never a tax from me,
> But never a tax from me."

_____ **16.** What events are described in the passage?

    (1) Revolutionary War
    (2) French and Indian War
    (3) Boston Tea Party
    (4) War of 1812

_____ **17.** Who is the island queen?

    (1) colonists   **(3)** Native Americans
    (2) queen of France   **(4)** queen of England

_____ **18.** The organization formed to represent Americans' interests and
challenge British control was

(1) minutemen
(2) Loyalists
(3) Continental Congress
(4) committee of correspondence

Base your answer to question 19 on the outline below and on your knowledge of social
studies.

Causes of the Revolutionary War
- Colonists' tradition of self-government
- Americans' desire for a separate identity from Britain
- Proclamation of 1763
- _____

_____ **19.** Which of the following would best complete the outline above?

(1) Long war with the British
(2) Self-government for the United States
(3) World recognition of United States independence
(4) Harsh British policies toward North America after 1763

_____ **20.** Why did the British march to Lexington and Concord?

(1) to have a meeting with Sam Adams and Paul Revere
(2) to announce new tax laws
(3) to seize and destroy weapons and arrest militia leaders
(4) to practice marching in formation

_____ **21.** The first battle of the Revolutionary War took place in

(1) Ticonderoga
(2) Bunker Hill
(3) Lexington
(4) Concord

_____ **22.** What was the significance of the Second Continental Congress?

(1) Several distinguished guests were delegates.
(2) They sent the Olive Branch petition to King George III.
(3) It created the first American flag.
(4) It was the first attempt to govern the united colonies.

_____ 23. What was the most important thing the Second Continental Congress did to help the colonies win the war?

(1) It established committees to communicate with Native Americans.
(2) It authorized the printing of money.
(3) It created the Continental Army to fight the British in an organized way.
(4) It elected the first president of the United States.

_____ 24. George Washington was the commander of

(1) the Sons of Liberty
(2) the British troops
(3) the Second Continental Congress
(4) the Continental Army

_____ 25. In *Common Sense*, Thomas Paine argued that

(1) the colonists should have paid taxes to Britain
(2) the war was a struggle for freedom that would affect all mankind
(3) it was silly to argue over taxation
(4) only when the colonists defeated the British would they be truly free

Base your answers to questions 26 and 27 on the excerpt below and on your knowledge of social studies.

"We hold these truths to be self-evident, that all men are created equal, that they are endowed by their Creator with certain unalienable Rights, that among these are Life, Liberty, and the pursuit of Happiness."
—*Preamble to the Declaration of Independence*

_____ 26. According to the Declaration of Independence, life, liberty, and the pursuit of happiness are considered

(1) unalienable rights   (3) human rights
(2) Constitutional rights   (4) legal rights

_____ 27. In Jefferson's time, who did the words "all men are created equal" apply to?

(1) all colonists
(2) only white men and women
(3) white men of English and European descent
(4) white men and Native Americans

_____ 28. American colonists who supported Britain were called

(1) Patriots   (3) Loyalists
(2) minutemen   (4) Separatists

Base your answers to questions 29 and 30 on the chart below and on your knowledge of social studies.

	British Army	Continental Army
Size of army	**32,000 men**	**230,000 men (only 20,000 at any time)**
Training	**Disciplined and well-trained**	**Inexperienced**
Supplies	**Well equipped**	**Poorly equipped**
Government	**Strong, central government**	**Weak and divided central government**
Support for war	**Limited support in England for war and its cost**	**Divided loyalties, many deserters**
Military strategy	**Traditional military strategy**	**Guerrilla warfare strategies**
Financial resources	**Wealth of resources from England**	**Support from France and Spain; foreign loans; personal financial support**
Motivation	**Fighting to retain colonies**	**Fighting to gain rights and freedoms**

_____ **29.** What is the best title for this chart?

   (1) Size and Skill of the British and Continental Armies
   (2) Comparison of Opposing Armies
   (3) Military Strategies of the British and Continental Armies
   (4) Motivations for the Revolutionary War

_____ **30.** Based on the information in the chart, which of the following statements is true?

   (1) The British army was much better trained and had vast resources.
   (2) The Continental Army was much more sophisticated than the British Army.
   (3) The British had strong support from British people and their government.
   (4) The Continental Army's tactics were based on traditional strategies.

_____ **31.** "I only regret that I have but one life to lose for my country."

   The above quote was said by

   (1) Nathan Hale
   (2) Thomas Paine
   (3) Patrick Henry
   (4) George Washington

Base your answers to questions 32 and 33 on the map below and on your knowledge of social studies.

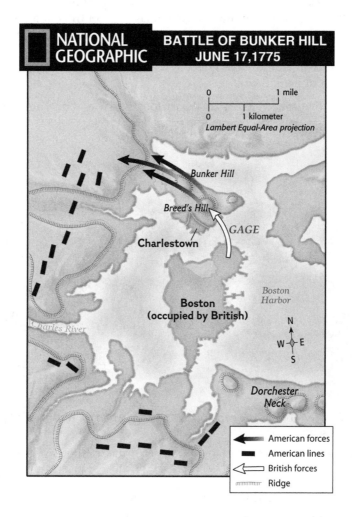

NATIONAL GEOGRAPHIC   BATTLE OF BUNKER HILL JUNE 17,1775

0   1 mile
0   1 kilometer
Lambert Equal-Area projection

Bunker Hill

Breed's Hill

GAGE

Charlestown

Boston Harbor

Boston (occupied by British)

N
W ◆ E
S

Charles River

Dorchester Neck

American forces
American lines
British forces
Ridge

32. What action did the American forces take after fighting the Battle of Bunker Hill?

(1) retreated
(2) advanced into Boston
(3) marched into Charlestown
(4) occupied Boston

33. In which direction did the British forces move when they left Boston?

(1) north   **(3)** south
(2) east   **(4)** west

_____ **34.** Why was it important for the Americans to win the Battle of Saratoga?

    (1) Victory would encourage France to support Britain.

    (2) Defeat would allow France to take over control of Saratoga.

    (3) Victory would prevent Britain from separating New England from the Middle Colonies.

    (4) Defeat would force Washington to resign as commander of the Continental Army.

Base your answers to questions 35–37 on the cartoon below and on your knowledge of social studies.

Library of Congress

_____ **35.** What symbol in the cartoon represents America in this 1779 political cartoon?

    (1) the rider on the horse   **(3)** the weapon in the rider's hand

    (2) the bucking horse   **(4)** the colonies are not represented

_____ **36.** Who might the rider on the horse represent?

    (1) King George III or other British leaders

    (2) George Washington

    (3) all European nations

    (4) Paul Revere

_____ **37.** What message is this cartoon presenting?

    (1) British forces would not quit until they crushed the Americans.

    (2) Americans should hold on tight and not allow the British to throw them.

    (3) Americans were filled with spirit as they fought for their independence from Britain.

    (4) The cartoon is just meant to make people laugh.

Base your answer to question 38 on the passage below and on your knowledge of social studies.

"I cannot say that I think you are very generous to the ladies, for, whilst you are proclaiming peace and good will to men, emancipating all nations, you insist upon retaining an absolute power over wives."

—Abigail Adams

_____ 38. What was Abigail Adams advocating in this letter to her husband?

(1) support for women who wanted to open their own businesses
(2) monetary compensation for women who lost their husbands in the war
(3) education for all people
(4) women's rights

_____ 39. How did the British prevent the Continental Army from receiving supplies and reinforcements?

(1) Their navy blockaded the American harbors.
(2) They bribed the French to turn over the Americans' supplies to them.
(3) They hired privateers to attack the American navy.
(4) They made a new law preventing ships in or out of the harbor.

_____ 40. Which battle convinced Britain that the war against the Americans was too costly?

(1) Battle at Charles Town
(2) Battle of Yorktown
(3) Battle at Vincennes
(4) Battle of Saratoga

_____ 41. What was the name of the peace treaty that ended the Revolutionary War?

(1) Treaty of Versailles
(2) Treaty of Yorktown
(3) Treaty of Greenville
(4) Treaty of Paris

_____ 42. One reason that Americans were able to win the Revolutionary War was that

(1) they had the help of German mercenaries
(2) they were fighting on their own ground
(3) their soldiers were better trained and equipped
(4) women fought alongside men

Part II: Constructed-Response Questions

DIRECTIONS: *Read the passage below. Then answer the questions based on the information in the passage and on your knowledge of social studies.*

41 colonists aboard the Mayflower crafted this agreement.

> Having undertaken for the Glory of God, and Advancement of the Christian Faith, and the Honour of our King and Country, a Voyage to plant the first Colony in the northern Parts of Virginia; Do by the Presents, solemnly and mutually, in the Presence of God and one another, covenant and combine ourselves together into a civil Body Politick, for our better Ordering and Preservation, and Furtherance of the Ends aforesaid: And by Virtue hereof do enact, constitute, and frame, such just and equal Laws, Ordinances, Acts, Constitutions, and Officers, from time to time, as shall be thought most meet and convenient for the general Good of the Colony; unto which we promise all due Submission and Obedience. In Witness whereof we have hereunto subscribed our names at Cape-Cod the eleventh of November, 1620.
> —*excerpt from the Mayflower Compact*

1. Why was the agreement created?

_____

_____

2. Why did the 41 men sign the compact?

_____

_____

3. Why was the compact important?

_____

_____

DIRECTIONS: Read the paragraph below. Then answer the questions based on the passage and on your knowledge of social studies.

> I am more convinced than ever of the necessity of discipline and system in the management of our affairs. I have heard several officers who have served under General Gates compare his army to a well-regulated family. The same gentlemen have compared Gen'l Washington's imitation of an army to an unformed mob. Look at the characters of both! The one [Gates] on the pinnacle of military glory—exulting in the success of schemes planned with wisdom, and executed with vigor and bravery. . . . See the other [Washington] outgeneraled and twice beaten. . . .
>   —*from a letter from Dr. Benjamin Rush to John Adams, October 21, 1777*

1. What is Benjamin Rush suggesting in his letter to John Adams?

   _____

   _____

2. Summarize Benjamin Rush's opinion about both General Gates and General Washington.

   _____

   _____

Part III: Document-Based Questions

This exercise is designed to test your ability to work with historical documents. It is similar to the document-based questions that you will see on the Intermediate-Level Test in Social Studies. While you are asked to analyze three historical documents, the exercise on the Intermediate-Level Test in Social Studies may include up to nine documents.

Some of the documents have been edited for the purposes of the question. As you analyze the documents, take into account the source of each document and any point of view that may be presented in the document.

Historical Context: Tensions between Britain and the colonies reached a critical point. It appeared as though the war for freedom was inevitable. Not all colonists, however, supported the war.

Task: Use information from the documents and your knowledge of social studies to answer the questions that follow each document in Part A. Your answers to the questions will help you write the Part B essay in which you will be asked:

> Various views about the need to take up arms against Britain were evident following the colonists' call for independence from England in July 1776. Discuss some of these views and the reasons for them.

Part A: Short-Answer Questions

DIRECTIONS: Analyze each document, and answer the questions that follow.

Document 1 Patrick Henry of Virginia, in his 1775 speech

> . . . Has Great Britain any enemy, in this quarter of the world, to call for all this accumulation of navies and armies? No, sir, she has none. They are meant for us: they can be meant for no other. They are sent over to bind and rivet upon us to those chains which the British ministry have been so long forging. And what have we to oppose them? Shall we try argument? Sir, we have been trying that for the last ten years . . . but it has been all in vain. . . .

1.*a* What view did Patrick Henry have regarding whether America should seek independence from Britain?

_____

_____

b What reasons did he give to support his view?

_____

_____

Document 2 from "The Congress," 1776 song

Ye Tories all rejoice and sing
Success to George our gracious King,
The faithful subjects tribute [praise] bring
And [denounce] the Congress.

Prepare, prepare, my friends prepare
For scenes of blood, the field of war;
To royal standard we'll repair,
And curse the haughty Congress.

Huzza! Huzza! and thrice Huzza!
Return peace, harmony and law!
Restore such times as once we saw
And bid adieu to Congress.

2.*a* Who do you think sang this song—Patriots or Loyalists? Why?

_____

_____

  b What did the people who sang this song want to do?

_____

_____

Document 3 Member of the Stockbridge tribe, from his 1775 speech given to the Massachusetts congress

> Brothers!
> You remember, when you first came over the great waters, I was great and you were little—very small. I then took you in for a friend, and kept you under my arms, so that no one might injure you. Since that time we have ever been true friends: there has never been any quarrel between us. But now our conditions are changed. You are become great and tall. You reach to the clouds. You are seen all around the world. I am become small—very little. . . .
> Brothers! I am sorry to hear of this great quarrel between you and old England. It appears that blood must soon be shed to end this quarrel. We never till this day understood the foundation of this quarrel between you and the country you came from. . . .

3.*a* Whose side is the speaker on—the Patriots or the Loyalists?

_____

_____

  b Why were the Native Americans in a difficult position in deciding which side
      to take?

_____

_____

Part B: Essay

DIRECTIONS: *Write a well-organized essay that includes an introduction, several paragraphs, and a conclusion. Use evidence from the three documents in the body of the essay. Support your response with relevant facts, examples, and details. Include additional outside information.*

> Various views about the need to take up arms against Britain were evident
> following the colonists' call for independence from England in July 1776.
> Discuss some of these views and the reasons for them.

Unit 4—A New Nation, *1777–1789*

Overview

After winning their independence, the thirteen states adopted new state constitutions. These new states recognized the need to form some kind of central government and adopted the Articles of Confederation in 1777. This was the first government of the United States. Though it was a central government, most power was centered in the states.

By 1787 the weaknesses of the Articles of Confederation were clear. After strong debate throughout the country, a new Constitution was ratified by all thirteen states. It was now time for the nation to elect leaders and begin the work of government.

With the ratification of the new Constitution, the United States was ready to face its many challenges. George Washington was unanimously elected as the first president. The first Congress established a federal court system. Ten amendments, known as the Bill of Rights, were added to the Constitution. Many of the nation's greatest challenges involved the national debt and the country's finances. Washington warned the nation about the dangers of political parties and getting the new nation involved in foreign affairs.

Essential Questions

As you prepare for the Intermediate-Level Test in Social Studies, ask yourself these essential questions:

- What were the weaknesses of the Articles of Confederation?

- Why were they made part of the Articles of Confederation?

- How does the United States Constitution limit the power of government?

- Why was the Bill of Rights created?

- How do the United States Constitution and the New York State Constitution compare and contrast?

Part I: Multiple-Choice Questions

DIRECTIONS: *Write the number of the answer that best completes the statement or answers the question.*

_____ 1. America's first constitution was

(1) the Republic
(2) the Treaty of Paris
(3) the Declaration of Independence
(4) the Articles of Confederation

_____ 2. What was the purpose of the Northwest Ordinance?

(1) to divide the Northwest Territory into as many smaller pieces of land as possible
(2) to prevent any of the 13 original states from purchasing the land
(3) to allow settlement of the Northwest Territory in a fair and orderly manner
(4) to protect land that originally belonged to Native Americans

_____ 3. Which of the following was a negative result of the Revolutionary War?

(1) great financial problems
(2) the Ordinance of 1785
(3) establishment of the Articles of Confederation
(4) a rise in the value of currency

_____ 4. Why did Northern states object to the Southern states wanting to include slaves in their population counts?

(1) Slaves were legally considered property.
(2) They didn't believe slaves should be considered as people.
(3) They didn't want the Southern states to have more representatives in the House.
(4) Representatives from the North thought that slaves should be given the right to vote.

_____ 5. The purpose of the Bill of Rights was to

(1) provide for states' rights
(2) describe the separation of powers
(3) protect individual rights
(4) provide for an army and navy

6. A system of government in which the people elect representatives to exercise power for them is called
   (1) socialism
   (2) a monarchy
   (3) a republic
   (4) communism

7. Which of the following was one reason for a new constitution?
   (1) to establish that all property belonged to the central government
   (2) to give some states greater power over others
   (3) to provide guidelines for a stronger central government
   (4) to outline a new set of rights for women

8. What was the result of the Great Compromise?
   (1) A grand committee was established to resolve disagreements between delegates.
   (2) A bill of rights would be included in the Constitution.
   (3) The power to approve taxes would remain with the states.
   (4) A two-house legislature would be established.

9. How many states had to approve the Constitution?
   (1) 13
   (2) 5
   (3) 10
   (4) 9

10. The belief that all people have natural rights and that government is based on an agreement between the people and the ruler was first described by
   (1) Baron de Montesquieu
   (2) John Locke
   (3) King George III
   (4) Daniel Shays

11. The sharing of power between the federal and state governments is called
   (1) anarchy
   (2) socialism
   (3) loyalism
   (4) federalism

Base your answers to questions 12 and 13 on the chart below and on your knowledge of social studies.

Powers of the Federal Government		
	Articles of Confederation	**United States Constitution**
Declare war; make peace	✔	✔
Coin money	✔	✔
Manage foreign affairs	✔	✔
Establish a postal system	✔	✔
Impose taxes		✔
Regulate trade		✔
Organize a court system		✔
Call state militias for service		✔
Protect copyrights		✔
Take other necessary actions to run the federal government		✔

12. Which document allowed the government to organize state militias?

   (1) Articles of Confederation
   (2) United States Constitution
   (3) both
   (4) neither

13. Which of the following best describes the difference between the two documents?

   (1) The Articles are shorter than the Constitution.
   (2) The Constitution gives the states more rights than the Articles.
   (3) The Constitution gives the federal government more powers than the Articles.
   (4) The Articles allowed the federal government to coin money; the Constitution did not.

_____ **14.** As set up by the United States Constitution, the three branches of government are legislative, executive, and

(1) judicial   (3) representative
(2) federal   (4) gubernatorial

_____ **15.** The legislative branch of government is made up of

(1) the cabinet departments
(2) the president and the vice president
(3) the Supreme Court and circuit courts
(4) the Senate and the House of Representatives

_____ **16.** The major role of the executive branch of government is

(1) to make the laws
(2) to carry out laws and policies
(3) to interpret the laws
(4) to keep any one branch from gaining power

_____ **17.** What is the purpose of a system of checks and balances?

(1) to keep any one state from acquiring too much land
(2) to prevent any changes to the constitution
(3) to set up a new banking system
(4) to keep any one branch from gaining too much power

_____ **18.** The secretary of state, the secretary of the treasury, the secretary of war, and the attorney general were all part of the

(1) State Department   (3) War Department
(2) cabinet   (4) Judicial Department

_____ **19.** The group of amendments added to the Constitution to protect the rights of individual liberty is the

(1) Judiciary Act   (3) cabinet
(2) Bill of Rights   (4) precedents

Base your answers to questions 20 and 21 on the statements below and on your knowledge of social studies.

> **Speaker A:** A society based on manufacturing develops dishonesty in people because a life of commerce makes people manipulate one another for gain.

> **Speaker B:** Manufacturing will help agriculture by freeing farmers from having to make the products they need both for farming and for daily life.

_____ **20.** Why does Speaker A dislike manufacturing?

(1) It makes people lazy.
(2) It doesn't pay well.
(3) It makes people dishonest.
(4) Factory jobs are more dangerous than farming.

_____ 21. Why does Speaker B believe that manufacturing will help agriculture?

    (1) because farmers will be free to concentrate on farming
    (2) because factories can produce tools farmers need
    (3) because manufacturers will buy products from farmers
    (4) because the country needs both manufacturing and agriculture

_____ 22. Alexander Hamilton planned to improve the nation's financial reputation by

    (1) paying off the national debt
    (2) selling government bonds
    (3) never borrowing money from foreign nations again
    (4) placing tariffs on American-made goods

_____ 23. What message did the end of the Whiskey Rebellion send to Americans?

    (1) The government was not willing to discuss changes to any laws.
    (2) The government felt that farmers should pay more taxes since they made the whiskey.
    (3) The government would not tolerate violent protests.
    (4) The government would not tolerate the making or drinking of whiskey.

_____ 24. What problem did the new government face in the West?

    (1) Native Americans and settlers clashed over land claims.
    (2) The terrain made settlement in the West difficult.
    (3) France wanted to occupy land in the West.
    (4) Native Americans charged high prices for the land.

_____ 25. When a nation remains neutral during times of war, it

    (1) tries to help end the conflict
    (2) supports whichever side seems to be winning
    (3) supports both sides involved in the conflict
    (4) does not take sides in the conflict

_____ 26. How many terms did Washington serve as president of the United States?

    (1) one
    (2) two
    (3) three
    (4) four

_____ 27. The first political parties to form were called

    (1) Federalists and Democrats
    (2) Federalists and Democratic-Republicans
    (3) Republicans and Democrats
    (4) Patriots and Democrats

Base your answer to question 28 on the flowchart below and on your knowledge of social studies.

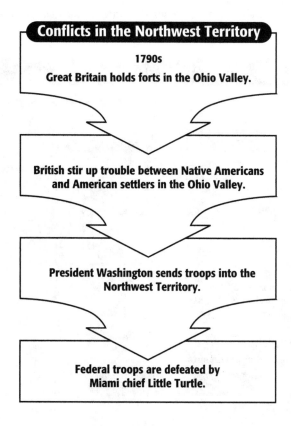

Conflicts in the Northwest Territory

1790s
Great Britain holds forts in the Ohio Valley.

British stir up trouble between Native Americans and American settlers in the Ohio Valley.

President Washington sends troops into the Northwest Territory.

Federal troops are defeated by Miami chief Little Turtle.

28. What action did Washington take in response to trouble in the Ohio Valley?

    (1) took over forts in the Ohio Valley

    (2) made a deal with Native Americans to fight the British

    (3) signed a treaty with the British

    (4) sent troops into the Northwest Territory

Part II: Constructed-Response Questions

DIRECTIONS: *Evaluate the chart below. Then answer the questions based on the information in the chart and on your knowledge of social studies.*

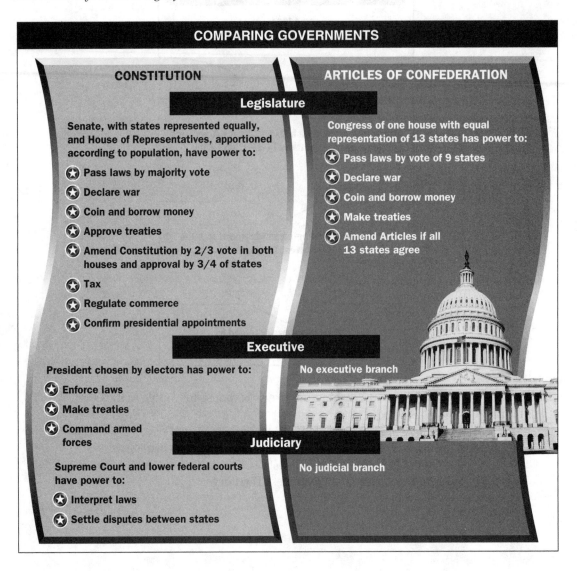

COMPARING GOVERNMENTS

CONSTITUTION

ARTICLES OF CONFEDERATION

Legislature

Senate, with states represented equally, and House of Representatives, apportioned according to population, have power to:

- ⭐ Pass laws by majority vote
- ⭐ Declare war
- ⭐ Coin and borrow money
- ⭐ Approve treaties
- ⭐ Amend Constitution by 2/3 vote in both houses and approval by 3/4 of states
- ⭐ Tax
- ⭐ Regulate commerce
- ⭐ Confirm presidential appointments

Congress of one house with equal representation of 13 states has power to:

- ⭐ Pass laws by vote of 9 states
- ⭐ Declare war
- ⭐ Coin and borrow money
- ⭐ Make treaties
- ⭐ Amend Articles if all 13 states agree

Executive

President chosen by electors has power to:

- ⭐ Enforce laws
- ⭐ Make treaties
- ⭐ Command armed forces

No executive branch

Judiciary

Supreme Court and lower federal courts have power to:

- ⭐ Interpret laws
- ⭐ Settle disputes between states

No judicial branch

1. According to this chart, which branches of government were added to the Constitution?

_____

_____

2. Based on this chart, who makes up the legislative branch of government?

_____

_____

3. According to this chart, how can the Constitution be amended?

_____

_____

DIRECTIONS: *Read the excerpt below. Then answer the questions based on the reading and on your knowledge of social studies.*

> Do you know that European birds have not half the melody of ours? Nor is their fruit half so sweet, nor their flowers half so fragrant, nor their manners half so pure, nor their people half so virtuous.
> —*from a letter by Abigail Adams, wife of John Adams,*
> *from England, to her sister*

1. How does Abigail Adams feel about America?

_____

_____

2. What do you think Abigail Adams meant when she wrote "nor their manners half so pure, nor their people half so virtuous"?

_____

_____

3. How do you think a European might have felt if he or she had read this part of the letter? Explain your answer.

_____

_____

Part III: Document-Based Questions

This exercise is designed to test your ability to work with historical documents. It is similar to the document-based questions that you will see on the Intermediate-Level Test in Social Studies. While you are asked to analyze three historical documents, the exercise on the Intermediate-Level Test in Social Studies may include up to nine documents.

Some of the documents have been edited for the purposes of the question. As you analyze the documents, take into account the source of each document and any point of view that may be presented in the document.

Historical Context: Even before the Revolutionary War, attempts were made to unite the colonies to form a federal government. These early documents helped shape the eventual Constitution of the United States.

Task: Use information from the documents and your knowledge of social studies to answer the questions that follow each document in Part A. Your answers to the questions will help you write the Part B essay in which you will be asked:

> Analyze the early attempts to form a federal government. Discuss which ideas in these documents were incorporated into the Constitution and which were rejected and why. What important themes do the documents have in common?

Part A: Short-Answer Questions

DIRECTIONS: Analyze each document, and answer the questions that follow:

Document 1 A committee, led by Benjamin Franklin, developed the Albany Plan of Union in 1754.

> It is proposed that humble application be made for an act of Parliament of Great Britain, by virtue of which one general government may be formed in America, including all the said colonies, within and under which government each colony may retain its present constitution, except in the particulars wherein a change may be directed by the said act, as hereafter follows. That the said general government be administered by a President-General, to be appointed and supported by the crown; and a Grand Council, to be chosen by the representatives of the people of the several Colonies met in their respective assemblies. . . .
>
> 8. That the assent [agreement] of the President-General be requisite [required] to all acts of the Grand Council, and that it be his office and duty to cause them to be carried into execution. . . .
>
> 13. That they raise and pay soldiers and build forts for the defence of any of the Colonies, and equip vessels of force to guard the coasts and protect the trade on the ocean, lakes, or great rivers, but they shall not impress men in any Colony, without the consent of the Legislature.
>
> 14. That for these purposes they have the power to make laws; and lay and levy such general duties, imposts, or taxes, as to them shall appear most equal and just (considering the ability and other circumstances of the inhabitants of several Colonies), and such as may be collected with least inconvenience to the people; rather discouraging luxury, than loading industry with unnecessary burdens.

1.*a* What powers did the Albany Plan of Union give to the federal government?

_____

_____

**   *b*** How would the British still have control over the colonists?

_____

_____

Document 2 In response to British Parliament's "Intolerable Acts" (harsh laws designed to punish Boston for resisting British authority), the First Continental Congress met in 1774. A committee drew up a declaration of rights, which is excerpted below.

> That the inhabitants of the English Colonies in North America, by the immutable laws of nature, the principles of the English constitution, and the several charters or compacts, have the following Rights:
>
> Resolved, N.C.D.
>
> 1. That they are entitled to life, liberty, and property, and they have never ceded to any sovereign power whatever, a right to dispose of either without their consent. . . .
>
> 4. That the foundation of English liberty, and of all free government, is a right in the people to participate in their legislative council: and as the English colonists are not represented . . . and cannot be properly represented, they are entitled to a free and exclusive power of legislation in their several provincial legislatures, where their right of representation can alone be preserved, in all cases of taxation and internal polity [government]. . . .
>
> 8. That they have a right peaceably to assemble, consider of their griev-ances, and petition the King. . . .
>
> 10. It is indispensably necessary to good government, and rendered essen-tial by the English constitution, that the constituent branches of the legislature be independent of each other. . . .

2.*a*   How might this document serve to unite the colonists in their growing desire for a separate identity from Britain?

_____

_____

  b   What rights does this document raise that were not claimed in the Albany Plan of Union?

_____

_____

Document 3 The thirteen colonies ratified the Articles of Confederation, which created the first federal government for the new nation.

> I.   The Stile of this Confederacy shall be "The United States of America."
>
> II.   Each state retains its sovereignty, freedom, and independence, and every power, jurisdiction, and right, which is not by this Confederation expressly delegated to the United States, in Congress assembled. . . .
>
> IV.   . . . The free inhabitants of each of these States . . . shall be entitled to all privileges and immunities of free citizens in the several states and the people of each state shall free ingress [enter] and regress [leave] to and from any other State. . . .
>
> VI.   No state shall engage in war without the consent of the United States in Congress assembled. . . .
>
> VIII.   All charges of war, and other expenses that shall be incurred for the common defense or general welfare . . . shall be defrayed out of a common treasury . . . The taxes for paying that proportion shall be laid and levied by the authority and discretion of the legislatures of the several States within the time agreed upon by the United States in Congress assembled.
>
> IX.   The United States in Congress assembled, shall have the sole and exclusive right and power of determining on peace and war . . .entering into treaties and alliances. . . .
>
> [It] shall also be the last resort on appeal in all disputes and differences now subsisting or that hereafter arise between two or more States. . . .[It] shall have the sole and exclusive right and power of regulating the alloy and value of coin struck by their own authority. . . .

3._a_ What were some of the major features of the government created by the Articles of Confederation?

_____

_____

  _b_ What were some of the weaknesses of the new government?

_____

_____

Part B: Essay

DIRECTIONS: Write a well-organized essay that includes an introduction, several paragraphs, and a conclusion. Use evidence from the three documents in the body of the essay. Support your response with relevant facts, examples, and details. Include additional outside information.

> Analyze the early attempts to form a federal government. Discuss which ideas in these documents were incorporated into the Constitution and which were rejected and why. What important themes do the documents have in common?

Unit 5—Growth and Expansion, *1789–1853*

Overview

In September 1796, Washington announced he would not seek a third term as president. John Adams, a Federalist, won the presidency by three votes. He faced problems with France and division within his own political party.

In 1800, Thomas Jefferson was chosen as the third president of the United States. One of the most important acts of Jefferson's presidency was the purchase of the Louisiana Territory. Significant problems arose as Britain and France went to war against each other.

James Madison was elected president in 1808. He faced continuing problems with Great Britain as well as threats from Native Americans in the West.

In the mid-1700s, inventors in Great Britain created machinery to perform some of the work involved in cloth making. These innovations led to changes, not only in industry, but also in the way people lived. These changes are known as the Industrial Revolution.

During the 1800s, Americans moved west of the Appalachian Mountains in increasing numbers. To support the movement of people and goods, roads and canals were built connecting the East with the Ohio River valley.

President Monroe issued a statement declaring that the United States would oppose any new European colonies in North and South America. His statement later became known as the Monroe Doctrine.

In a hotly disputed election that was decided by the House of Representatives, John Adams became president in 1824. Andrew Jackson won the presidential elections of 1828 and 1832. During this time, many issues continued to divide the country.

As Americans moved westward, they came into more conflict with Native Americans. Settlers wanted the federal government to move Native Americans in the Southeast to land west of the Mississippi River. Many relocated, but many others did not survive the journey.

In the first half of the nineteenth century, Americans spread westward across the continent. As more settlers moved into the Oregon Territory, the United States and Britain clashed over the northern border with Canada. Land in Texas was offered to people who were willing to bring their families to settle there. When the Mexican government began placing limits on Texas, it sought to become independent. After a series of battles, Texas became part of the United States in 1845.

Many Americans believed in Manifest Destiny—the United States' right to the land all the way to the Pacific. The late 1840s brought the discovery of gold, which brought thousands to California.

In the first half of the nineteenth century, industrialization and technology changed life in America. The North was characterized by a growing factory system, larger cities, and a wave of immigration. The South remained largely rural and agricultural. By 1860 there were great differences between the North and South.

In the 1800s, a spirit of reform swept through America. The abolitionist movement and women's movement also grew during this time.

Essential Questions

As you prepare for the Intermediate-Level Test in Social Studies, ask yourself these essential questions:

- How did the first political parties arise?
- What challenges did President John Adams face?
- How did John Marshall strengthen the Supreme Court?
- What was the significance of the Louisiana Purchase?
- What were the causes and effects of the War of 1812?
- What were the causes and effects of the Industrial Revolution?
- What were the causes and effects of westward expansion?
- How did President Monroe's foreign policy differ from his predecessor's?
- What political changes occurred under President Jackson?
- What were the causes and effects of the Indian Removal Act?
- How did the idea of Manifest Destiny contribute to the nation's growth?
- How did the United States acquire Texas, New Mexico, and California?
- What advances in technology shaped the economy of the North?
- Why did the economy of the South depend on agriculture?
- Who were the important leaders of various reform movements?

Part I: Multiple-Choice Questions

DIRECTIONS: Write the number of the answer that best completes the statement or answers the question.

_____   1.   Who was elected president after George Washington?
    (1) Thomas Jefferson
    (2) Alexander Hamilton
    (3) James Madison
    (4) John Adams

Base your answer to question 2 on the cartoon below and on your knowledge of social studies.

Federalist Roger Grimswald attacks Republican Matthew Lyon with a cane. Lyon seizes a pair of fire tongs and fights back.

_____ 2. How are the members of Congress reacting to the fight?
  (1) They are horrified.
  (2) They are angry.
  (3) They are amused.
  (4) They are sad.

_____ 3. President Jefferson believed that
  (1) the federal government should become more powerful
  (2) the size and power of the federal government should be reduced
  (3) the size of the military should be increased
  (4) the size of the military should be reduced

_____ 4. The Supreme Court case of _Marbury_ v. _Madison_ established that
  (1) federal law took precedence over state law in interstate transportation
  (2) the Supreme Court had the right to rule on acts of the other branches of government
  (3) the elastic clause allowed Congress to do more than it was expressly authorized to do in the Constitution
  (4) segregation in public facilities was unconstitutional

_____ 5. The United States purchased the Louisiana Territory from

     (1) Germany

     (2) Spain

     (3) England

     (4) France

Base your answers to questions 6–8 on the map below and on your knowledge of social studies.

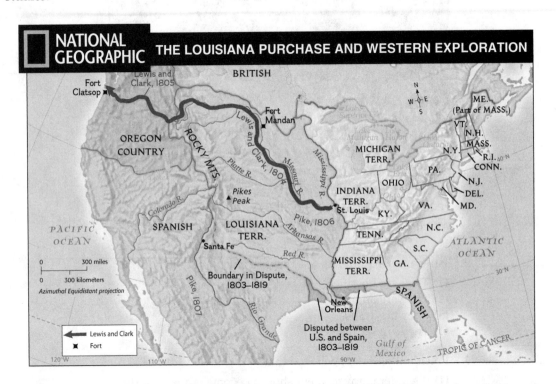

_____ 6. What geographical barrier did Lewis and Clark have to cross in order to reach the Pacific Ocean?

     (1) Rocky Mountains

     (2) Colorado River

     (3) Mississippi River

     (4) Arkansas River

_____ 7. What was the eastern border of the Louisiana Purchase?

     (1) Ohio River

     (2) Missouri River

     (3) Lake Michigan

     (4) Mississippi River

_____ 8. Why was the Louisiana Purchase significant?

(1) It inspired people to want to move west.
(2) It removed Spanish influence in the United States.
(3) It helped forge a military partnership with France.
(4) It allowed the United States to stretch to the Pacific Ocean.

_____ 9. Sacagawea was a Shoshone woman who

(1) traveled the entire length of the Mississippi River
(2) helped to discover Grand Peak
(3) served as a guide on the Louisiana expedition
(4) found new trails across the Rocky Mountains

_____ 10. The purpose of the Embargo Act was to

(1) establish closer trade ties with Britain and France
(2) ban all imports from and exports to foreign countries
(3) force people to serve in the British navy
(4) remain neutral in the French-British conflict

_____ 11. "The Star-Spangled Banner" was composed during

(1) the Spanish-American War
(2) the Civil War
(3) the Revolutionary War
(4) the War of 1812

_____ 12. The act of forcing people to serve in the navy is called

(1) embargo
(2) impressment
(3) neutrality
(4) tribute

_____ 13. Which statement best describes the impact of the Embargo Act?

(1) It destroyed commerce with other nations.
(2) It avoided war with Britain.
(3) It increased American exports.
(4) It increased American trade with Latin America.

_____ 14. Why was France in conflict with America during this period?

(1) France was siding with the British in disputes.
(2) France was selling goods to Britain.
(3) France was seizing American ships and selling their goods.
(4) France wanted some of America's territories.

Base your answer to question 15 on the quote below and on your knowledge of social studies.

"They have driven us from the sea to the lakes—we can go no farther."
                                                          —*Tecumseh*

_____ 15. Who was Tecumseh speaking about?

   (1) General William Henry Harrison
   (2) French trappers
   (3) Iroquois people
   (4) white settlers

_____ 16. Who was the United States battling in the War of 1812?

   (1) Britain and France
   (2) Canada
   (3) Britain and their Native American allies
   (4) France and their Native American allies

_____ 17. Which of the following is an example of how the Americans were unprepared for the War of 1812?

   (1) The troops did not have adequate supplies.
   (2) They expected to get support from Native Americans.
   (3) There were not enough troops and they were poorly trained.
   (4) They were defeated at Lake Erie.

_____ 18. Loyalty to one's country is called

   (1) secessionism
   (2) nationalism
   (3) colonialism
   (4) loyalism

_____ 19. The peace agreement that ended the War of 1812 was the

   (1) Treaty of Greenville
   (2) Treaty of Ghent
   (3) Treaty of Paris
   (4) Treaty of New Orleans

_____ 20. New England was an ideal location for the development of mills because

   (1) it had many rivers to provide the waterpower needed to run machines
   (2) farming had begun to be less profitable
   (3) there were many mills and factories in England
   (4) the people were talented weavers

Base your answers to questions 21 and 22 on the time line below and on your knowledge of social studies.

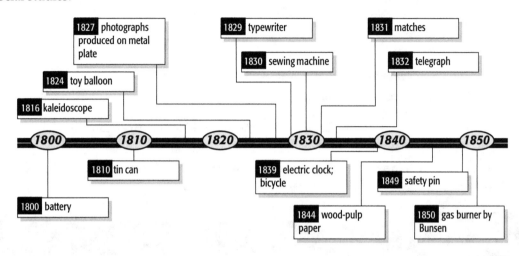

_____ **21.** How many inventions are recorded on the time line from 1810 to 1830?

    (1) two   **(3)** six

    (2) five   **(4)** ten

_____ **22.** When were the electric clock and the bicycle invented?

    (1) 1830   **(3)** 1842

    (2) 1839   **(4)** 1847

_____ **23.** How did the invention of the cotton gin affect cotton production?

    (1) It reduced the size of crops the planters could raise.

    (2) It made the cleaning of cotton quicker and more efficient.

    (3) It increased the size of farms in the Northeast.

    (4) It had no effect on the production of cotton.

_____ **24.** In general, the women who worked in the New England textile mills were

    (1) protected by labor laws

    (2) overworked and underpaid

    (3) taking jobs from men

    (4) paid an excellent wage

_____ **25.** The use of interchangeable parts increased production because

    (1) factories had more machines for people to work

    (2) owners needed more skilled labor to create them

    (3) they were more complicated to fix

    (4) they made machine repair easier

_____ **26.** The waterway built to connect Albany and Buffalo, New York, was the

(1) Hudson River

(2) Erie Canal

(3) New York Canal

(4) Lake Champlain

_____ **27.** The years following the War of 1812 were marked by

(1) a sense of national unity

(2) widespread western immigration

(3) understanding between Americans and Native Americans

(4) continued conflict with European nations

Base your answers to questions 28 and 29 on the map below and on your knowledge of social studies.

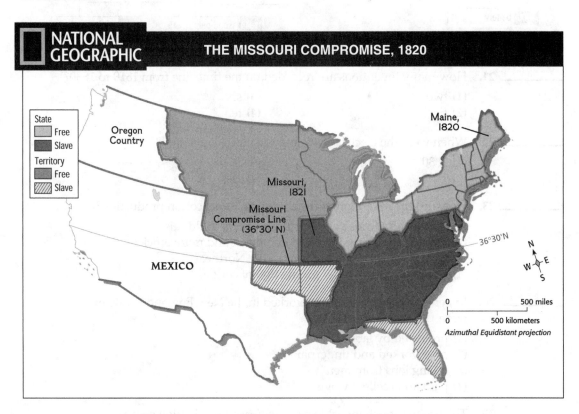

NATIONAL GEOGRAPHIC

THE MISSOURI COMPROMISE, 1820

State
Free
Slave

Territory
Free
Slave

Oregon Country

Maine, 1820

Missouri, 1821

Missouri Compromise Line (36°30′ N)

MEXICO

36°30′N

0   500 miles

0   500 kilometers

Azimuthal Equidistant projection

28. The Missouri Compromise was reached to settle a dispute concerning

(1) taxes   (3) agriculture
(2) slavery   (4) foreign policy

29. According to the Missouri Compromise, Maine was admitted to the Union as

(1) a slave state   (3) an industrial state
(2) a free state   (4) part of Massachusetts

30. The Monroe Doctrine affected foreign policy by

(1) opposing any new European colonies in the Americas
(2) preventing President Monroe from running for re-election
(3) encouraging new European colonies in the Americas
(4) increasing the size of the U.S. army and navy

31. In the election of 1824, Andrew Jackson claimed to speak for

(1) America's favorite sons
(2) Americans who had been raised in poverty
(3) wealthy merchants and bankers
(4) the common man

Base your answer to question 32 on the chart below and on your knowledge of social studies.

Election of 1824

Candidate	Electoral Vote	Popular Vote	House Vote
Jackson	99	153,544	7
Adams	84	108,740	13
Crawford	41	46,618	4
Clay	37	47,136	–

32. Which candidate received the most electoral votes?

(1) Jackson   (3) Crawford
(2) Adams   (4) Clay

33. Under the terms of the Twelfth Amendment to the Constitution, who selects the president when no candidate receives the majority of electoral votes?

(1) the House of Representatives   (3) the Electoral College
(2) the Senate   (4) the Supreme Court

_____ **34.** An important factor in the election of Andrew Jackson in 1828 was the

   (1) support of Henry Clay
   (2) support of the Federalists
   (3) ratification of the Twelfth Amendment
   (4) increase in the number of eligible voters

_____ **35.** How did Andrew Jackson try to get the people's support in the election of 1828?

   (1) He surrounded himself with a group of trusted advisors.
   (2) He made up the nickname "Old Hickory" for himself.
   (3) He promised greater protection and benefits for wealthy Americans.
   (4) He accused John Quincy Adams of betraying the American people.

Base your answers to questions 36 and 37 on the cartoon below and on your knowledge of social studies.

BORN TO COMMAND.

KING ANDREW THE FIRST.

_____ **36.** What does the artist want readers to think of President Jackson?

   (1) that he is assuming the powers of a king
   (2) that he is vetoing too many laws
   (3) that he is interpreting the Constitution
   (4) that he is doing a good job

_____ **37.** What symbols does the artist use to represent the United States?

   (1) the crown and scepter   **(3)** the clothes Jackson is wearing
   (2) the veto in Jackson's hand   **(4)** the eagle and the Constitution

38. The term *suffrage* refers to the right

(1) to vote   (3) to own slaves

(2) to own property   (4) to pay taxes

39. The system in which candidates are chosen by closed and secret committees that are made up of members of Congress is called

(1) the spoils system   (3) a bureaucracy

(2) a caucus system   (4) a landslide election

40. Southern planters did not approve of the high protective tariff of 1828 because

(1) it forced merchants to lower the prices on their goods

(2) it made goods imported from Europe more expensive

(3) it was an illegal fee charged to consumers by merchants

(4) it would force the Southern states to secede

41. What was the main purpose of the Indian Removal Act?

(1) to force Native Americans to resettle in the Southeast

(2) to make the area west of the Mississippi River more suitable for farming

(3) to remove President Jackson from office

(4) to force Native Americans to resettle west of the Mississippi River

Base your answers to questions 42 and 43 on the passage below and on your knowledge of social studies.

"Brothers! I have listened to many talks from our Great Father. When he first came over the wide waters, he was but a little man. . . . But when the white man had warmed himself before the Indians' fire and filled himself with their hominy, he came very large. With a step he bestrode the mountains and his feet covered the plains and the valleys. His hand grasped the eastern and the western sea, and his head rested on the moon. Then he became our Great Father. Brothers, I have listened to a great many talks from our Great Father. But they always began and ended in this—'Get a little further; you are too near me.'"

—*Speckled Snake, elder of the Creek nation, 1829*

42. What events are described?

(1) colonial settlement

(2) the forced migration of Native Americans

(3) the first Thanksgiving

(4) the War of 1812

43. What is Speckled Snake's opinion of those he speaks of?

(1) He admires them.   (3) He envies them.

(2) He feels bad for them.   (4) He feels angry and distrustful.

_____ **44.** The "Trail of Tears" describes the forced migration of

(1) the Cherokee people
(2) the Chickasaw people
(3) the Creek people
(4) the Choctaw people

_____ **45.** What was the response of the Seminoles when they were removed from their lands?

(1) They took action in the United States court system.
(2) They willingly moved to new territory.
(3) They attacked the white settlements on their land.
(4) They demanded payment before they left.

_____ **46.** Which of the following was a result of the Panic of 1837?

(1) Businesses closed and people lost their jobs.
(2) Congress created Indian Territory.
(3) Southern cotton prices rose to record highs.
(4) Land values rose sharply.

_____ **47.** According to the principle of *laissez-faire*

(1) the government should deposit its money in private banks
(2) the government should interfere with private business as little as possible
(3) business owners should get interest-free government loans
(4) the national debt should be eliminated

_____ **48.** William Henry Harrison's log cabin campaign was most similar to the campaign of

(1) Martin Van Buren   **(3)** Andrew Jackson
(2) John Tyler   **(4)** John C. Calhoun

_____ **49.** Which of the following expresses an opinion about Andrew Jackson?

(1) Jackson served two terms as president.
(2) He spoke out against South Carolina's Nullification Act.
(3) Because of Jackson, the United States has the best system of filling government positions.
(4) Jackson supported the Indian Removal Act.

_____ **50.** In the mid-1800s, Manifest Destiny referred to the idea that the purpose of the United States was

(1) to extend its borders to the Pacific Ocean
(2) to extend its borders to the Mississippi River
(3) to acquire European lands
(4) to acquire the unclaimed lands of South America

Base your answers to questions 51 and 52 on the time line below and on your knowledge of social studies.

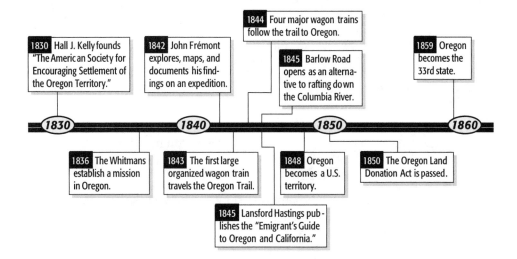

_____ 51. What period of time is covered on the time line?

    (1) 1820–1860
    (2) 1830–1880
    (3) 1810–1850
    (4) 1830–1860

_____ 52. When was the first wagon train organized to travel on the Oregon Trail?

    (1) 1834
    (2) 1843
    (3) 1844
    (4) 1852

Base your answer to question 53 on the quote below and on your knowledge of social studies.

> "The power of Santa Anna is to be met here, or in the colonies; we had better meet them here than to suffer a war of devastation to rage in our settlements."
> —*Commander William Travis*

_____ 53. What is Commander Travis saying in this statement?

    (1) Victory for the Americans is assured.
    (2) Mexican forces are retreating.
    (3) They must defeat the Mexicans in Texas.
    (4) The Mexicans are advancing into the colonies.

_____ **54.** Which of the following was a cause of the United States' war with Mexico?

    (1) Mexico refused to sell Oregon to the United States.

    (2) The United States and Mexico disagreed over the location of each other's borders.

    (3) Mexico annexed Texas illegally.

    (4) President Polk disagreed with Manifest Destiny.

_____ **55.** Which of the following was the result of the discovery of gold in California?

    (1) Gold was discovered in the Black Hills of the Dakotas.

    (2) Western expansion and foreign immigration increased.

    (3) California was annexed as a slave state.

    (4) The United States went to war with Mexico.

Base your answer to question 56 on the cartoon below and on your knowledge of social studies.

_____ **56.** What idea is the cartoon presenting?

    (1) People rushed west to find gold.

    (2) People were anxious to travel on the Oregon Trail.

    (3) Mormons were rushing to settle Utah.

    (4) Women liked to race horses.

_____ **57.** The mechanical reaper, the steel-tipped, and the thresher resulted in

    (1) increased harvests for Western farmers
    (2) increased harvests for Southern farmers
    (3) growth of factories
    (4) the growth of agricultural imports

Base your answer to question 58 on the pie charts below and on your knowledge of social studies.

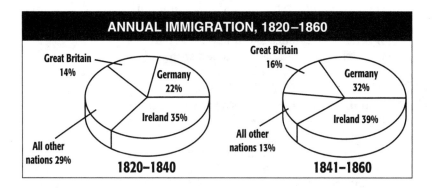

_____ **58.** Between 1820 and 1860, the greatest number of immigrants to the United States came from

    (1) Mexico and China
    (2) Italy and Spain
    (3) Russia and Poland
    (4) Germany and Ireland

_____ **59.** How did the cotton gin affect the economy of the South?

    (1) Southerners did not want industry to develop in the South.
    (2) Southerners flocked to northern factories.
    (3) The demand for enslaved African Americans increased.
    (4) Enslaved African Americans were freed.

_____ **60.** Little industry developed in the South because of the lack of capital. *Capital* refers to

    (1) non-slave laborers
    (2) money to invest in businesses
    (3) manufactured goods
    (4) the market for manufactured goods

_____ **61.** Which of the following was a result of the Second Great Awakening?

    (1) Missionary work increased.
    (2) Church membership decreased.
    (3) Involvement in social reform decreased.
    (4) Civil disobedience increased.

_____ **62.** In the 1850s, which of the following was an accepted principle of public education?

    (1) Girls and boys should study the same subjects.
    (2) School should be free and supported by public taxes.
    (3) School attendance should be up to parents.
    (4) Teachers should be unmarried women.

_____ **63.** Labor unions were formed to

    (1) improve workers' wages and work conditions
    (2) protect factory owners from being sued
    (3) make stricter rules for workers
    (4) prevent children from taking jobs from adults

_____ **64.** An abolitionist was a person who sought to

    (1) reform education   **(3)** rid the states of slavery
    (2) ban alcohol   **(4)** promote civil disobedience

Base your answer to question 65 on the passage below and on your knowledge of social studies.

> "What, to the American slave, is your Fourth of July? I answer: a day that reveals to him, more than all other days in the year, the gross injustice and cruelty to which he is the constant victim. To him, your celebration is a sham . . . your national greatness, swelling vanity; your sounds of rejoicing are empty and heartless . . . your shouts of liberty and equality, hollow mockery."
> —*Frederick Douglass*

_____ **65.** Why does the Fourth of July represent injustice to Douglass?

    (1) It celebrates freedom and there is no freedom for African Americans.
    (2) He is free and others are not.
    (3) He wasn't born in the United States.
    (4) He is a slave.

_____ **66.** Which of the following statements is true?

    (1) Elizabeth Blackwell opened the first high school for girls.
    (2) Women gained the right to vote at the Seneca Falls Convention.
    (3) The women's movement ended at the Seneca Falls Convention.
    (4) The fight to end slavery helped to spark the women's movement.

Part II: Constructed-Response Questions

DIRECTIONS: Read the excerpt below and answer the questions that follow using the space provided. Base your answers to the questions on the reading below and on your knowledge of social studies.

> On Tuesday evening we fell in with a detachment of the poor Cherokee Indians. . . . That poor despised people are now on their long and tedious march to their place of destination beyond the Mississippi River. . . . We found them in the forest camped for the night by the road side, comfortable—if comfortable they might be in a December night, and under a severe fall of rain accompanied with heavy wind. . . . We learned . . . that many of the aged Indians were suffering extremely from the fatigue of the journey, and the ill health consequent upon it. . . . We learned from the inhabitants on the road where the Indians passed that they buried fourteen to fifteen at every stopping place—and they made a journey of ten miles per day only on an average. One aged Indian . . . was accosted on arriving in a little village in Kentucky by . . . one of Jackson's men. The aged Chieftain . . . said, "I thought Jackson my best friend. But ah! Jackson no serve me right. Your country no do me justice now."
> —*A native of Maine who witnessed the Trail of Tears, 1838*

1. Describe the conditions in which the writer found this group of Cherokee.

_____

_____

2. How does the aged Chieftain feel about the forced relocation of his people?

_____

_____

3. How do you think the writer feels about the forced relocation of the Cherokee?

_____

_____

_____

DIRECTIONS: Read the excerpt below and answer the questions that follow using the space provided. Base your answers to the questions on the reading below and on your knowledge of social studies.

> The consequences of a speedy removal will be important to the United States, to individual states, and to the Indians themselves. . . . It puts an end to all possible danger of collision between the authorities of the general and state governments on account of the Indians. . . . It will separate the Indians from immediate contact with settlements of whites; free them from the power of the states; enable them to pursue happiness in their own way and under their own rude institutions. . . . Toward the aborigines [natives] of the country no one can indulge a more friendly feeling than myself, or would go further in attempting to reclaim them from their wandering habits and make them a happy, prosperous people. . . . May we not hope, therefore, that all good citizens . . . will unite in attempting to open the eyes of those children of the forest to their true condition, and by a speedy removal to relieve them from all the evils, real or imaginary, present or prospective, with which they may be supposed to be threatened.
>
> —*President Andrew Jackson in a message to Congress, 1830*

1. According to Jackson, what are two reasons that a speedy removal of the Native Americans is advantageous to the parties involved?

   _____

   _____

2. How does Jackson justify removing Native Americans from their homelands?

   _____

   _____

3. Does Jackson really indulge a "friendly feeling" toward Native Americans? Explain.

   _____

   _____

   _____

Part III: Document-Based Questions

This exercise is designed to test your ability to work with historical documents. It is similar to the document-based questions that you will see on the Intermediate-Level Test in Social Studies. While you are asked to analyze three historical documents, the exercise on the Intermediate-Level Test in Social Studies may include up to nine documents.

Some of the documents have been edited for the purposes of the question. As you analyze the documents, take into account the source of each document and any point of view that may be presented in the document.

Historical Context: The idea of reform—the drive to improve society and the lives of Americans—grew during the mid-1800s. Reformers set out to improve the lives of the disadvantaged, including enslaved people, women, and the urban poor.

Task: Use information from the documents and your knowledge of social studies to answer the questions that follow each document in Part A. Then use your answers to help you write the essay in Part B in which you will be asked to:

> Describe the social conditions that caused dissatisfaction among many women between the 1820s and the 1850s. What difference did age, race, and social class play in the lives of women living during this period? Explain.

Part A: Short-Answer Questions

DIRECTIONS: Analyze the documents and answer the short-answer questions that follow.

Document 1 Catherine Beecher, writing in support of higher education for women in 1829

> It is to mothers, and to teachers, that the world is to look for the character which is to be enstamped on each succeeding generation, for it is to them that the great business of education is almost exclusively committed. And will it not appear by examination that neither mothers nor teachers have been properly educated for their profession. What is the profession of a Woman? Is it not to form immortal minds, and to watch, to nurse, and rear the bodily system . . . upon the order and regulation of which, the health and well-being of the mind so greatly depends? But . . . have you ever devoted any time and study, in the course of your education, to any preparation for these duties?

1.*a* What does Beecher believe is the most important job of mothers and teachers?

_____

_____

  b Why does Beecher believe that mothers and teachers are poorly prepared for their job?

_____

_____

c What subjects do you think Beecher would have women study? Why?

_____

_____

_____

Document 2 Written in 1898, these reminiscences are by Harriet Hanson Robinson, a woman who had worked in the cotton mills of Lowell, Massachusetts, in the late 1830s, when she was 11 years old.

> The working-hours of all the girls extended from five o'clock in the morning until seven in the evening, with one-half hour for breakfast and for dinner. . . . One of the first strikes of cotton-factory operatives that ever took place in this country was that in Lowell, in October 1836. When it was announced that the wages were to be cut down, great indignation was felt, and it was decided to strike, *en masse.* This was done. The mills were shut down, and the girls went in procession from their several corporations to the "grove" on Chapel Hill, and listened to "incendiary" speeches from early labor reformers. One of the girls stood on a pump, and gave vent to the feelings of her companions in a neat speech, declaring that it was their duty to resist all attempts at cutting down the wages. This was the first time a woman had spoken in public in Lowell, and the event caused surprise and consternation among her audience.

2.*a* Why did these female workers strike?

_____

_____

b What message did the female worker give to her audience?

_____

_____

c What effect did the female worker's speech have on the audience?

_____

_____

Document 3 Born a slave and later set free, Sojourner Truth became a traveling religious preacher and abolitionist. Having discovered the women's rights movement, she spoke at the Ohio Women's Convention in 1851.

> Well, children, where there is so much racket there must be something out of kilter. I think that 'twixt the Negroes of the South and the women at the North, all talking about rights, the white men will be in a fix pretty soon. But what's all this here talking about? That man over there says that women need to be helped into carriages, and lifted over ditches, and to have the best place everywhere. Nobody ever helps me into carriages, or over mud-puddles, or gives me any best place! And ain't I a woman?

3.*a* How does Truth feel about the women's rights movement? How do you know?

_____

_____

_____

  b How do you think Truth's speech affected those who heard her at the Ohio Women's Convention?

_____

_____

Part B: Essay

DIRECTIONS: *Write a well-organized essay that includes an introduction, several paragraphs, and a conclusion. Use evidence from the documents in the body of the essay. Support your response with relevant facts, examples, and details. Include additional outside information.*

> Describe the social conditions that caused dissatisfaction among many women between the 1820s and the 1850s. What difference did age, race, and social class play in the lives of women living during this period? Explain.

Unit 6—Civil War and Reconstruction, *1850–1877*

Overview

Between 1819 and 1860, events led the United States closer to a civil war. The major issue in these events was slavery in the territories. The Supreme Court's *Dred Scott* decision contributed to the controversy over slavery. By 1860 many Southerners felt that they could no longer stay in the Union. The election of Republican Abraham Lincoln led several Southern states to secede and form the Confederate States of America. Its president was Jefferson Davis.

When Confederate forces fired on Fort Sumter, President Lincoln issued a call for troops and the Civil War began. From 1861 to 1865 the United States was torn apart by a great civil war. On the home front, both Northerners and Southerners faced deprivations and hardships. Overall, the North's industrial economy boomed during the war, while the Southern economy suffered terribly. On January 1, 1863, President Lincoln's Emancipation Proclamation took effect, freeing all enslaved people in the Confederacy. On April 9, 1865, when Robert E. Lee surrendered to Ulysses S. Grant at Appomattox Court House in Virginia, the conflict ended.

As the Civil War drew to a close, President Lincoln and the leaders in Congress began to develop plans to bring the South back into the nation. The assassination of President Lincoln threw the country into mourning and delayed the swift rebuilding of the nation.

A key part of Reconstruction was the establishment of civil rights for African Americans. Some whites wanted to limit the rights of African Americans. They accomplished this through the passage of laws called black codes. Other groups used intimidation and violence to prevent freed men and women from exercising their rights. The Compromise of 1877 brought about the end of Reconstruction.

Essential Questions

As you prepare for the Intermediate-Level Test in Social Studies, ask yourself these essential questions:

- How was the debate over slavery related to the admission of new states?
- What was the result of the *Dred Scott* decision?
- Why did states in the South secede from the Union?
- Why were border states important during the Civil War?
- What advantages did the North and the South have prior to the war?
- What strategies did the North and South use to try to win the war?
- Why did Lincoln issue the Emancipation Proclamation?
- What was the debate over Reconstruction?
- How were the rights of African Americans increased?
- How were the rights of African Americans limited?
- How did Reconstruction change life in the South?

Part I: Multiple-Choice Questions

DIRECTIONS: *Write the number of the answer that best completes the statement or answers the question.*

_____ 1. Having a strong loyalty to a particular region of the country is known as

(1) stateism   (3) secessionism
(2) regionalism   (4) sectionalism

_____ 2. The Free-Soil Party was created

(1) to avoid having to take a stand on slavery
(2) to take a stand opposing the extension of slavery
(3) to fight for the abolition of slavery
(4) to advocate for the extension of slavery

_____ 3. The purpose of the Missouri Compromise was to

(1) ensure a balance of slave and free states
(2) ensure an increase in the number of free states
(3) ensure an increase in the number of slave states
(4) abolish slavery in states in which it was legal

_____ 4. The Wilmot Proviso stated that

(1) the government did not have the authority to regulate slavery
(2) slavery should be abolished in the District of Columbia
(3) slavery should be prohibited in any lands acquired from Mexico
(4) states that allowed slavery should secede from the Union

Base your answer to question 5 on the quote below and on your knowledge of social studies.

"I would rather hear of natural blasts and mildew, war, pestilence, and famine, than to hear gentlemen talk of secession."
—*Daniel Webster*

_____ 5. Webster thought that secession

(1) could be avoided by compromise
(2) was inevitable
(3) would be good for the country
(4) would be worse than war

_____ 6. An effect of the Compromise of 1850 was

(1) the slave trade was abolished in the District of Columbia
(2) there were restrictions on slavery in New Mexico
(3) California was admitted as a slave state
(4) the New Mexico-Texas border dispute favored Texas

_____ 7. The 1850 law that required all citizens to help catch runaway slaves was called

(1) the Fugitive Slave Act   (3) the Underground Slave Act
(2) the Runaway Slave Act   (4) the Uncle Tom Act

Base your answer to question 8 on the quotation below and on your knowledge of social studies.

" . . . [T]he two great divisions of society are not rich and poor, but white and black; and all the former, the poor as well as the rich, belong to the upper classes, and are respected and treated as such."

—*Senator John Calhoun*

_____ 8. What part of Calhoun's statement most indicates his bias?

(1) All whites are members of the upper class.
(2) There is a division in society.
(3) The division is between rich and poor.
(4) The division is between black and white.

_____ 9. The plan to allow each territory to vote on slavery was known as

(1) territorial sovereignty
(2) popular sovereignty
(3) popular choice
(4) electoral choice

Base your answers to questions 10 and 11 on the chart below and on your knowledge of social studies.

Number of Enslaved People in Northern and Southern States: 1790–1850		
Year	**Number of Enslaved People in Northern States**	**Number of Enslaved People in Southern States**
1790	164,500	529,500
1810	223,200	907,400
1830	273,800	1.57 million
1850	303,800	2.18 million

_____ **10.** What trend does the information in the table show?

(1) The number of slaves in the Northern states was increasing while in the South it was decreasing.

(2) The number of slaves in the Northern states was decreasing while in the South it was increasing.

(3) The number of slaves was increasing in both regions.

(4) The number of slaves was decreasing in both regions.

_____ **11.** Based on this information, why do you think the South was more dependent on enslaved people for labor?

(1) Their economy was based on manufacturing.

(2) There were more people living in the South.

(3) Their economy was based on agriculture.

(4) They needed enslaved people to work in factories.

_____ **12.** The Kansas-Nebraska Act provided that the Kansas and Nebraska territories

(1) could not become states   (3) were open to slaveholding

(2) would become slave states   (4) would become free states

_____ **13.** The name of the abolitionist who led an attack against slavery supporters in Kansas is

(1) John Brown   (3) Harriet Beecher Stowe

(2) Stephen A. Douglas   (4) Harriet Tubman

_____ **14.** Which statement about the effect of _Uncle Tom's Cabin_ is true?

(1) Many people in the South became more opposed to slavery.

(2) Many more people in the North became supporters of slavery.

(3) Many people in the North criticized the book.

(4) Many more people in the North became opposed to slavery.

_____ **15.** In the _Dred Scott_ decision, the Supreme Court ruled that

(1) neither Congress nor voters could prohibit slavery in any territory

(2) living on free soil made Dred Scott a free man

(3) slavery was unconstitutional

(4) only voters could prohibit slavery in a territory

_____ **16.** Which statement describes Stephen A. Douglas's stand on slavery?

(1) He supported it, but thought that the issue should be decided by popular sovereignty.

(2) He was strongly opposed to it and wanted the practice eliminated.

(3) He strongly supported it and thought it should be allowed to spread.

(4) He disliked it, but thought that national controversy over it should be avoided.

_____ 17. Which of the following statements about the Lincoln-Douglas debates is true?

(1) Lincoln won the debates because he was much better known than Douglas.
(2) Douglas stated that African Americans should be fully equal to whites.
(3) Following the debates, Douglas lost the election but gained a national reputation.
(4) Following the debates, Lincoln lost the election but gained a national reputation.

_____ 18. What was the result of John Brown's raid on Harpers Ferry?

(1) The raid was successful, but Brown was badly injured.
(2) Brown was defeated, but he went on to become an abolitionist.
(3) Brown was convicted of treason and murder and was hanged.
(4) The raid was successful and led to a slave rebellion.

_____ 19. The split in the Democratic Party in 1860 was caused by

(1) the belief that the North needed more representation
(2) the division over the issue of slavery
(3) the belief that the South needed more representation
(4) the division over the issue of protective tariffs

Base your answer to question 20 on the outline below and on your knowledge of social studies.

        I. _____

        A. Abraham Lincoln was elected president.
        B. South Carolina secedes from the Union.
        C. Confederate forces demanded the surrender of Fort Sumter.

_____ 20. What would be the best title for the outline above?

(1) Causes of Secession
(2) Events Leading to Civil War
(3) Events of 1858
(4) Results of Lincoln-Douglas Debates

_____ 21. How did Lincoln plan to prevent secession?

(1) He threatened to drive the states out of the Union.
(2) He promised to uphold the right to slavery in the South.
(3) He vowed to hold federal property in the South and enforce the laws of the United States.
(4) He threatened to abolish slavery in states that seceded.

_____ **22.** The first state to secede from the Union was

    (1) Texas   **(3)** California

    (2) Georgia   **(4)** South Carolina

_____ **23.** Who was chosen to be president of the Confederate States of America?

    (1) Abraham Lincoln   **(3)** Thomas Jefferson

    (2) Jefferson Davis   **(4)** Stephen A. Douglas

_____ **24.** How did the Civil War begin?

    (1) U.S. forces attacked Fort Sumter.

    (2) Confederate forces shot President Lincoln.

    (3) U.S. forces shot President Davis.

    (4) Confederate forces attacked Fort Sumter.

Base your answer to question 25 on the graph below and on your knowledge of social studies.

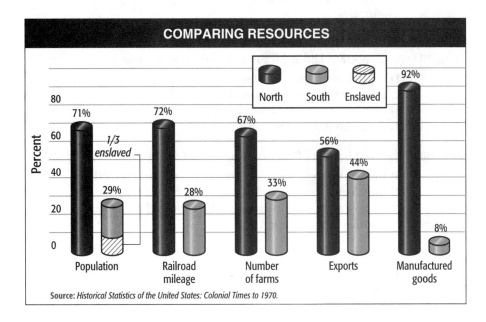

Source: *Historical Statistics of the United States: Colonial Times to 1970.*

_____ **25.** In what two areas did the North have the greatest advantage over the South?

    (1) population and railroad mileage

    (2) railroad mileage and number of farms

    (3) number of farms and exports

    (4) railroad mileage and manufactured goods

_____ **26.** The Confederacy's strong belief in states' rights

    (1) made the delivery of supplies to its troops more efficient
    (2) increased the Confederacy's ability to fight the war effectively
    (3) decreased the Confederacy's ability to fight the war effectively
    (4) made the delivery of supplies to its troops difficult

_____ **27.** For Southerners, the primary aim of the Civil War was

    (1) to reunite the Union and the Confederacy
    (2) to take control of the Mississippi River
    (3) to open up trade with Europe
    (4) to preserve their way of life, which included slavery

_____ **28.** Why was Lincoln's naval blockade of Southern ports important?

    (1) It tied up Confederate ships.
    (2) It made Northern ports vulnerable to attack.
    (3) It prevented the South from exporting and importing goods and supplies.
    (4) It forced the Confederate armies to surrender.

_____ **29.** An important Union strategy for winning the war was the plan to

    (1) capture plantation owners
    (2) take over the exportation of cotton
    (3) gain control of the Mississippi River
    (4) draft slaves into the army

_____ **30.** The First Battle of Bull Run was significant because

    (1) the Southern victory was shocking and unexpected
    (2) the Northern victory struck a blow to the South
    (3) it showed that the war would be shorter than expected
    (4) it took place on Union soil

_____ **31.** The battle between the *Monitor* and the *Merrimack*

    (1) was the first battle of the Civil War
    (2) resulted in both ships being sunk
    (3) was the last battle of the Civil War
    (4) marked a new age in naval warfare

_____ **32.** Gaining control of the Mississippi River was important for the Union army because

    (1) it would mean that the North won the war
    (2) it would give the Union control of New Orleans
    (3) it would split the Confederacy in two
    (4) it would make it easier for the South to ship goods

_____ **33.** The single bloodiest day of the Civil War was the Battle of

(1) Antietam

(2) Chancellorsville

(3) Shiloh

(4) Atlanta

_____ **34.** One major result of the Emancipation Proclamation was

(1) slaves in the border states were given their freedom

(2) the Confederacy decided to support the Proclamation

(3) all slaves in the United States were given their freedom

(4) Britain and France decided not to support the Confederacy

_____ **35.** One of the best-known African American regiments was the

(1) 801st Kentucky   (3) 61st New York

(2) 54th Massachusetts   (4) 2nd Cavalry Maryland

_____ **36.** What was the effect of the Thirteenth Amendment to the Constitution?

(1) It permitted African Americans to serve in the army.

(2) It abolished slavery in the United States.

(3) It ended the Civil War.

(4) It gave African Americans the right to vote.

Base your answer to question 37 on the outline below and on your knowledge of social studies.

    I.   Financing the War

   A. Impose new taxes

   B. Issue bonds to raise money

   C. _____

_____ **37.** Which of the following best completes the outline above?

(1) Sell more goods overseas

(2) Import more goods

(3) Print paper money

(4) Sell government lands

_____ **38.** How was the concept of total war different from earlier strategies?

(1) Total war included attacks on land, on sea, and from the air.

(2) Total war affected civilians as well as soldiers.

(3) Total war used every available soldier.

(4) Total war used more modern weapons.

Base your answer to question 39 on the passage below and on your knowledge of social studies.

"It is for us the living . . . to be here dedicated to the great task remaining before us . . . that these dead shall not have died in vain—that this nation, under God, shall have a new birth of freedom—and that government of the people, by the people, for the people shall not perish from the earth."
    —*Abraham Lincoln, the Gettysburg Address, 1863*

_____ 39. What did Lincoln mean with his words?

(1) The Union should surrender to the Confederates.
(2) The war was too costly and should be ended.
(3) The war had gone on too long to end it without a victory.
(4) The Union had to win the war to preserve the country and honor those who had already died.

_____ 40. The agency that supplied food, education, transportation, and medical services to African Americans after the Civil War was the

(1) Agency of Free Men   (3) Fisk Society
(2) Society of Free Men   (4) Freedmen's Bureau

_____ 41. The Fifteenth Amendment to the Constitution protects

(1) African Americans' right to vote
(2) the denial of constitutional privileges to citizens without due process of law
(3) the institution of slavery
(4) the right to privacy

_____ 42. Which of the following statements about the Civil Rights Act of 1866 is true?

(1) It granted full citizenship to African Americans.
(2) It denied the federal government the power to protect African Americans' rights.
(3) It gave states the right to pass black codes.
(4) It upheld the 1857 *Dred Scott* decision.

_____ 43. Which of the following statements best describes the impact of Reconstruction?

(1) It helped the South recover and create a new, industrial economy.
(2) It was a complete success.
(3) It was a complete failure.
(4) It helped the South recover and rebuild its agricultural economy.

_____ **44.** The poll tax and the literacy tax

(1) were put into effect as part of the Fifteenth Amendment
(2) had no impact on African Americans' voting rights in the South
(3) restricted African Americans' voting rights in the South
(4) supported African Americans' voting rights in the South

_____ **45.** By the 1890s, the Southern states passed Jim Crow laws in order to

(1) give equal rights to African Americans
(2) create a segregated society
(3) make sure slavery never took hold again
(4) increase cotton production

_____ **46.** The Supreme Court case that established the doctrine of "separate but equal" was

(1) _Marbury_ v. _Madison_   **(3)** _Lincoln_ v. _Douglas_
(2) _Dred Scott_   **(4)** _Plessy_ v. _Ferguson_

_____ **47.** The major failure of Reconstruction was that it

(1) led to a period of decreased farm production
(2) led to a period of economic inflation
(3) did not give true freedom to African Americans
(4) failed to impeach President Johnson

Part II: Constructed-Response Questions

DIRECTIONS: *Answer the questions that follow using the space provided. Base your answers to the questions on the cartoon below and on your knowledge of social studies.*

1. Who are the two men shown pulling at the map of the United States?

   _____

   _____

2. What does each of the men named above want?

   _____

   _____

   _____

3. What uniform is the figure in the middle wearing? What is he trying to prevent?

   _____

   _____

DIRECTIONS: *Answer the questions that follow the written document using the space provided. Base your answers to the questions on the reading below and on your knowledge of social studies.*

> . . . What, to the American slave, is your Fourth of July? I answer: a day that reveals to him, more than all other days in the year, the gross injustice and cruelty to which he is the constant victim. To him, your celebration is a sham; your boasted liberty, an unholy license; your national greatness, swelling vanity; your sounds of rejoicing are empty and heartless; your denunciation of tyrants, brass-fronted impudence; your shouts of liberty and equality, hollow mockery; your prayers and hymns, your sermons and thanksgivings, with all your religious parades and solemnity, are, to Him, mere bombast, fraud, deception, impiety, and hypocrisy—a thin veil to cover up crimes which would disgrace a nation of savages. . . . There is not a nation on the earth guilty of practices more shocking and bloody than are the people of the United States at this very hour. Go where you may, search where you will . . . and you will say with me that, for revolting barbarity and shameless hypocrisy, America reigns without a rival.
> —*Frederick Douglass, speaking in New York on July 4, 1852*

1. Douglass's speech stunned his audience. Why do you think they were stunned?

   _____

   _____

2. How does Douglass feel the United States compares with other countries of the world?

   _____

   _____

3. Why do you think Douglass felt safe saying what he did in New York?

   _____

   _____

   _____

Part III: Document-Based Questions

This exercise is designed to test your ability to work with historical documents. It is similar to the document-based questions that you will see on the Intermediate-Level Test in Social Studies. While you are asked to analyze three historical documents, the exercise on the Intermediate-Level Test in Social Studies may include up to nine documents.

Some of the documents have been edited for the purposes of the question. As you analyze the documents, take into account the source of each document and any point of view that may be presented in the document.

Historical Context: During the years surrounding the Civil War, the federal and state government passed several pieces of legislation that addressed the rights and abilities of African Americans to participate in civic life.

Task: Use information from the documents and your knowledge of social studies to answer the questions that follow each document in Part A. Then use your answers to help you write the essay in Part B in which you will be asked:

> Civil rights issues were paramount during the years surrounding the Civil War. Discuss how, during this period, the federal and state legislatures both protected and denied the rights of African Americans.

Part A: Short-Answer Questions

DIRECTIONS: Analyze the documents and answer the short-answer questions that follow.

Document 1 The Emancipation Proclamation, 1863

> . . . That on the 1st day of January, in the year of our Lord 1863, all persons held as slaves within any state or designated part of a state, the people whereof shall then be in rebellion against the United States, shall be then, thenceforward, and forever free; and the Executive Government of the United States, including the military and naval authority thereof, will recognize and maintain the freedom of such persons, and will do no act or acts to repress such persons, or any of them, in any efforts they may make for their actual freedom. . . .
>
> . . . And I further declare and make known that such persons, of suitable condition will be received into the armed service of the United States. . . .

1.*a* Why did the Emancipation Proclamation not actually free any enslaved people?

_____

_____

b What effect did Lincoln hope the Proclamation would have on the enslaved?

_____

_____

Document 2 Constitution of the United States, Amendment 13 (1865)

> **Section 1**
>
> Neither slavery nor involuntary servitude, except as a punishment for crime whereof the party shall have been duly convicted, shall exist within the United States, or any place subject to their jurisdiction.
>
> **Section 2**
>
> Congress shall have power to enforce this article by appropriate legislation.

2.*a* What was the purpose of Amendment 13?

_____

_____

  b What is the significance of Section 2 of the amendment?

_____

_____

_____

Document 3 Black Code Laws, Mississippi State Legislature, 1865

> *An act to regulate the relation of master and apprentice, as relates to freedmen, free negroes, and mulattoes.*
>
> SECTION 1. . . . It shall be the duty of all sheriffs, justices of the peace, and other civil officers of the several counties in this State, to report . . . all freedmen, free negroes, and mulattoes, under the age of eighteen . . . who are orphans, or whose parent or parents have not the means or who refuse to provide for and support said minors; and thereupon it shall be the duty of said probate court to order the clerk of said court to apprentice said minors to some competent and suitable person. . . .
>
> SEC. 2. . . . [S]aid apprentice shall be bound by indenture, in case of males, until they are twenty-one years old, and in case of females until they are eighteen years old.
>
> SEC. 3. . . . In the management and control of said apprentices, said master or mistress shall have the power to inflict such moderate corporeal chastisement as a father or guardian is allowed to inflict on his or her child or ward at common law. . . .
>
> SEC. 4. . . . If any apprentice shall leave the employment of his or her master or mistress, without his or her consent, said master or mistress may pursue and recapture said apprentice, and bring him or her before any justice of the peace of the county, whose duty it shall be to remand said apprentice to the service of his or her master or mistress. . . .

3._a_ How did the laws restrict the rights of African Americans?

_____

_____

_____

_b_ How were the black code laws similar to slavery?

_____

_____

_____

Part B: Essay

DIRECTIONS: *Write a well-organized essay that includes an introduction, several paragraphs, and a conclusion. Use evidence from the documents in the body of the essay. Support your response with relevant facts, examples, and details. Include additional outside information.*

> Civil rights issues were paramount during the years surrounding the Civil War. Discuss how, during this period, the federal and state legislatures both protected and denied the rights of African Americans.

Unit 7—Reshaping the Nation, *1858–1914*

Overview

As the California Gold Rush was ending, mining expeditions discovered gold and other precious metals in other parts of the West. The Homestead Act, railroads, and new farming methods all drew settlers to the Great Plains. Often these settlers came into conflict with the Native Americans who had made their homes there for centuries. Many years of violence ended with the conflict at Wounded Knee. The event marked the end of armed conflict between whites and Native Americans.

Although farming expanded following the Civil War, problems for farmers also grew. Several attempts were made to form organizations to improve the lives of farm families.

In the period following the Civil War, developments in technology and business changed the daily lives of Americans. The expansion of railroad lines allowed the movement of goods to take place more quickly and inexpensively, helping other industries to thrive, and paving the way for American industry to expand into the West. The industrial growth of the late 1800s created new jobs, but many of these jobs were in noisy, unhealthy, dangerous factories. Labor unions formed to demand better pay and working conditions from employers.

In the mid-1880s the pattern of immigration to the United States began to change. "New" immigrants arrived from eastern and southern Europe as well as from Mexico and Asia. People poured into the cities faster than housing could be built to accommodate them. Rapid urban growth created problems with sanitation, public health, and crime. By the turn of the century, government and business leaders and reformers believed that for the nation to progress, the people needed more schooling. Public schools, colleges, and universities all increased their enrollments.

In the late 1800s many Americans called for reform. They focused on urban problems, government, and business. The efforts of the woman suffrage movement were realized in 1920 when the Nineteenth Amendment was ratified, granting women the right to vote. When Theodore Roosevelt became president in 1901, he introduced progressive reforms to the White House, which were continued by presidents Taft and Wilson. For some Americans, however, the reforms of the Progressive Movement were not enough. Nonwhite, non-Protestant, and non-native residents often faced discrimination and, on some occasions, violence.

Essential Questions

As you prepare for the Intermediate-Level Test in Social Studies, ask yourself these questions:

- How did development of the railroads affect the nation?
- How did settlers acquire land on the Great Plains?
- Why did the government force Native Americans onto reservations?
- What problems did farmers face in the late 1800s?
- Why did the development of large corporations bring both benefits and problems?
- What were the goals of labor unions?

- How did the arrival of new immigrants change American society?

- What problems did cities face in the late 1800s?

- Why was education more available to Americans?

- What were the developments of the Progressive Movement?

- How did President Theodore Roosevelt take on big business?

Part I: Multiple-Choice Questions

DIRECTIONS: Write the number of the answer that best completes the statement or answers the question.

_____ 1. The deposit of silver-bearing ore discovered in Nevada in 1859 was the
   (1) Carson River Lode   (3) Pikes Peak Lode
   (2) Comstock Lode   (4) Silverado Lode

_____ 2. Which of the following was an effect of the discovery of gold and silver on western development?
   (1) It led to the destruction of many railroads.
   (2) It spurred the growth of the stock exchange in the West.
   (3) It speeded the flow of settlers who developed thriving communities.
   (4) It led to a decreased population as thousands fled the area.

_____ 3. Boomtowns often became ghost towns when
   (1) the nearby mines no longer yielded ore
   (2) people found out their homes were haunted
   (3) railroads were built through them
   (4) women and children began moving there

Base your answers to questions 4 and 5 on the line graph below and on your knowledge of social studies.

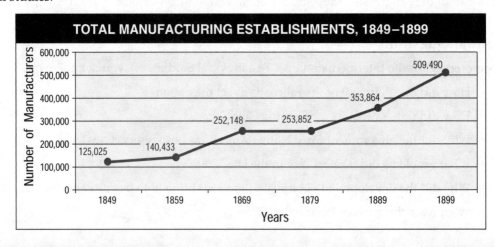

TOTAL MANUFACTURING ESTABLISHMENTS, 1849–1899

Number of Manufacturers
1849: 125,025
1859: 140,433
1869: 252,148
1879: 253,852
1889: 353,864
1899: 509,490

Years

_____ **4.** Approximately how many more manufacturing establishments were there in 1879 than in 1849?

    (1) 50,000
    (2) 200,000
    (3) 100,000
    (4) 125,000

_____ **5.** What was the likely result of the increase in manufacturing establishments on prices of goods?

    (1) They went up.
    (2) They went down.
    (3) They stayed the same.
    (4) There was a glut of goods.

_____ **6.** Texas cattle suddenly increased in value in the mid-1800s when

    (1) the government began regulating the prices of beef
    (2) new railroads allowed for the shipment of cattle to the North and East
    (3) people in the North and East started eating large quantities of beef
    (4) there was a shortage of prime beef in the far West

_____ **7.** Which of the following led to the end of the Cattle Kingdom?

    (1) There was not enough ranch land.
    (2) The price of beef fell.
    (3) Hot temperatures killed many cattle.
    (4) Cowhands got involved in violence.

_____ **8.** By 1881, more than 40,000 Exodusters moved to Kansas because

    (1) they had heard about the cheap land and pleasant climate there
    (2) there was an abundance of jobs available in the many new factories
    (3) the end of Reconstruction ended federal protection for African Americans in former slave states
    (4) they had plenty of money with which to start new farms and businesses

_____ **9.** Settlers on the Great Plains built homes from sod because

    (1) there were no trees and, therefore, no logs
    (2) they lacked tools with which to cut trees into lumber
    (3) sod homes were cooler in summer and warmer in winter
    (4) they couldn't afford to build homes from bricks or logs

Base your answers to questions 10 and 11 on the map below and on your knowledge of social studies.

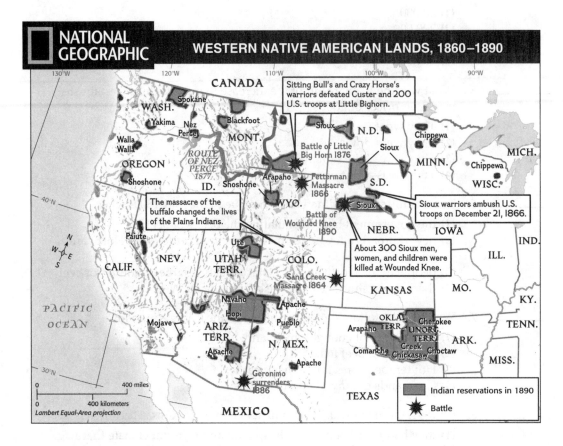

NATIONAL GEOGRAPHIC

WESTERN NATIVE AMERICAN LANDS, 1860–1890

_____ **10.** In what state did the Battle of Little Bighorn take place?

(1) Arizona Territory

(2) South Dakota

(3) Montana

(4) Colorado

_____ **11.** Which Native American nationals resettled in present-day Oklahoma?

(1) Apache, Navaho, and Hopi

(2) Cherokee, Creek, Choctaw, Chickasaw, Comanche, and Arapaho

(3) Sioux and Chippewa

(4) Shoshone, Yakima, and Walla Walla

_____ **12.** Why were buffalo important to Native Americans on the Great Plains?

   (1) Buffalo showed the Plains Indians where to find food.
   (2) Buffalo showed the Plains Indians where to find water.
   (3) The Plains Indians worshipped the buffalo.
   (4) Buffalo meat was their main source of food.

_____ **13.** Railroad companies hired hunters to kill buffalo for which reason?

   (1) to feed the crews building the railroad
   (2) to sell the meat to butchers in the East
   (3) to use the hides as shelter
   (4) to sell the meat to Native Americans

_____ **14.** What was the goal of the Dawes Act of 1887?

   (1) to encourage Native Americans to become farmers and American citizens
   (2) to discourage Native Americans from moving onto reservations
   (3) to make sure that there would always be enough reservation land
   (4) to keep Native American children out of white-run schools

_____ **15.** After the Civil War, farmers blamed their troubles on which of the following?

   (1) the lack of support from politicians
   (2) the cheap price of transportation
   (3) the high cost of purchasing seeds and fertilizer
   (4) the lack of loans available from bankers

_____ **16.** The reforms of the Populist Party appealed mostly to

   (1) politicians
   (2) wealthy factory owners
   (3) the common people
   (4) freed African Americans

_____ **17.** The Populist Party wanted to base the nation's currency on

   (1) gold
   (2) greenbacks
   (3) free silver
   (4) credit

Base your answers to questions 18 and 19 on the map below and on your knowledge of social studies.

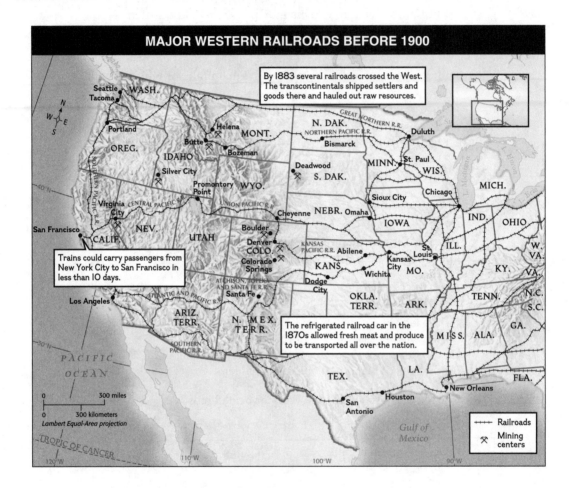

MAJOR WESTERN RAILROADS BEFORE 1900

By 1883 several railroads crossed the West. The transcontinentals shipped settlers and goods there and hauled out raw resources.

Trains could carry passengers from New York City to San Francisco in less than 10 days.

The refrigerated railroad car in the 1870s allowed fresh meat and produce to be transported all over the nation.

_____ **18.** Which railroad connected Los Angeles to New Orleans?

(1) Atlantic and Pacific
(2) Southern Pacific
(3) Kansas Pacific
(4) Union Pacific

_____ **19.** Which railroads would a traveler use from St. Louis to Virginia City?

    (1) Southern Pacific and Northern Pacific
    (2) Great Northern and Northern Pacific
    (3) Atchison, Topeka, and Santa Fe
    (4) Kansas Pacific, Union Pacific, and Central Pacific

_____ **20.** The age of air travel began when

    (1) Charles Lindbergh flew solo across the Atlantic Ocean in 1927
    (2) the Wright brothers achieved flight at Kitty Hawk in 1903
    (3) Louis Blériot flew across the English Channel in 1909
    (4) the first plane flew nonstop across the Atlantic Ocean in 1919

_____ **21.** Automobiles could be produced more quickly and cheaply as a result of

    (1) the assembly line
    (2) the discovery of petroleum
    (3) the automatic circuit breaker
    (4) the use of child labor

Base your answers to questions 22 and 23 on the time line below and on your knowledge of social studies.

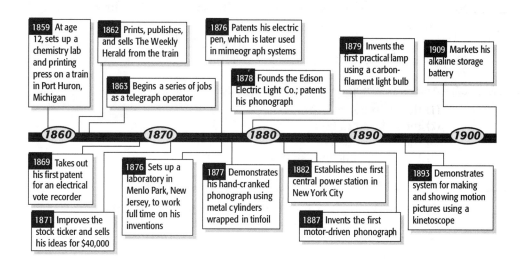

_____ **22.** When did Thomas Edison set up a power station in New York City?

    (1) 1877
    (2) 1879
    (3) 1882
    (4) 1893

_____ 23. In which ten-year period did Edison make the most inventions? Include patents.

(1) 1860–1870
(2) 1870–1880
(3) 1880–1890
(4) 1890–1900

_____ 24. Which of the following lists the economic factors of production?

(1) land, labor, capital
(2) capital, labor, dividends
(3) land and labor
(4) capital and labor

_____ 25. Which of the following statements best describes the United States economy from the end of the Civil War to 1900?

(1) Banks made huge profits while other businesses failed.
(2) It experienced an era of unmatched economic growth.
(3) It endured a period of widespread unemployment.
(4) Business ventures declined because of mass production.

_____ 26. A group of companies managed by the same board of directors is called a

(1) corporation   (3) stock exchange
(2) trust   (4) monopoly

_____ 27. Andrew Carnegie was the leading figure in the growth of

(1) the oil industry
(2) the railroad industry
(3) the steel industry
(4) the automobile industry

_____ 28. The lack of competition caused by trusts and monopolies

(1) hurt consumers by raising the prices of goods and services
(2) helped consumers by lowering the prices of goods and services
(3) had no effect on consumers
(4) gave consumers more choice in the marketplace

Base your answer to question 29 on the political cartoon below and on your knowledge of social studies.

_____ **29.** How does the cartoonist use size to make his point of view?

    (1) He shows the power the trusts have over the politicians.
    (2) He shows the trusts are bigger than the U.S. government.
    (3) He shows the trusts are too big for their own good.
    (4) He shows the politicians are uninterested in the trusts.

_____ **30.** Which of the following was a result of the industrial growth of the late 1800s?

    (1) Factories got smaller and more personal.
    (2) Fewer new jobs were created.
    (3) Luxuries were only affordable by the very wealthy.
    (4) Necessities became more affordable.

_____ **31.** In the late 1800s, which industry employed more women than any other?

    (1) the steel industry   **(3)** the food industry
    (2) the oil industry   **(4)** the textile industry

Base your answer to question 32 on the passage below and on your knowledge of social studies.

"We want eight hours [i.e., an eight-hour workday] and nothing less. We have been accused of being selfish, and it has been said that we will want more; that last year we got an advance of ten cents and now we want more. We do want more. You will find that a man generally wants more . . . You ask a working-man, who is getting two dollars a day, and he will say that he wants ten cents more . . . while the man who has his millions will want every thing he can lay his hands on and then raise his voice against the poor devil who wants ten cents more a day."

—*Samuel Gompers*

_____ 32. What is the topic sentence in this excerpt?
   (1) We have been accused of being selfish . . .
   (2) The man who has his millions will want every thing he can lay his hands on and then raise his voice against the poor devil who wants ten cents more a day.
   (3) You will find that a man generally wants more.
   (4) We do want more.

_____ 33. What is Gompers's purpose in this passage?
   (1) He is pushing for a shorter workday and better wages for workers.
   (2) He is criticizing rich men.
   (3) He is calling workers selfish.
   (4) He is calling for a strike.

_____ 34. The Knights of Labor differed from most labor unions because it
   (1) represented skilled workers in certain crafts and trades
   (2) recruited workers who had been turned away from trade unions
   (3) met openly and did not keep its membership secret
   (4) kept out women, African Americans, and immigrants

_____ 35. The system in which unions represent workers in negotiating with management is called
   (1) going on strike
   (2) collective bargaining
   (3) workers' rights
   (4) mass production

_____ 36. Business owners hired strikebreakers to
   (1) break up violent strikes
   (2) replace striking workers
   (3) restore order during strikes
   (4) strengthen labor unions

_____ 37. The International Ladies' Garment Workers Union pushed for safer working conditions as a result of

(1) the Triangle Shirtwaist Factory fire
(2) the Pullman Strike
(3) the Haymarket Riot
(4) the Homestead Strike

_____ 38. In the mid-1800s, the largest groups of immigrants to the United States came from

(1) northern Europe
(2) eastern and southern Europe
(3) Mexico
(4) China and Japan

Base your answers to questions 39 and 40 on the tables below and on your knowledge of social studies.

Manufacturing Establishments: Top Five States in 1870	
State	**Number of Manufacturing Establishments**
Pennsylvania	37,200
New York	36,206
Ohio	22,773
Massachusetts	13,212
Illinois	12,597

Foreign-born Population: Top Six States in 1870	
State	**Number of Foreign-born Residents**
New York	1,138,353
Pennsylvania	543,309
Illinois	515,198
Ohio	372,493
Wisconsin	364,499
Massachusetts	353,319

_____ 39. What correlation can be made between the statistics in the two tables?

(1) The number of manufacturing jobs had nothing to do with immigrant populations.
(2) Wisconsin had no manufacturing jobs.
(3) The five biggest manufacturing states have large immigrant populations.
(4) The more manufacturing jobs a state had, the larger the immigrant population.

_____ 40. What conclusion can be drawn from this correlation?

(1) Immigrants opened many manufacturing operations.
(2) Immigrants settled in cities where there were many manufacturing jobs.
(3) Immigrants avoided manufacturing jobs.
(4) Immigrants came to the city, then factories opened up.

_____ 41. The term *assimilate* is best defined as

(1) the act of leaving one's homeland
(2) the ability to speak two languages
(3) the desire to blend into a larger culture
(4) the desire to maintain one's old language and customs

_____ 42. The goal of the nativist movement was to

(1) blame immigrants for increasing crime
(2) obtain better living conditions for immigrants
(3) protect the rights of Native Americans
(4) oppose and place restrictions on immigration

_____ 43. Tenement buildings, improved transportation, and bridge-building all contributed to

(1) a rise in crime
(2) the growth of cities
(3) the boom in immigrant populations
(4) a decline in farming

_____ 44. Which one of the following fields are William Randolph Hearst and Joseph Pulitzer most closely associated with?

(1) journalism   (3) music
(2) philanthropy   (4) art

_____ 45. One goal of reformers in the late 1800s to early 1900s was to

(1) fight patronage, also known as the "spoils system"
(2) increase the power of trusts and monopolies
(3) decrease tariffs to make imported goods more affordable
(4) prevent suffrage for women

Base your answer to question 46 on the cartoon below and on your knowledge of social studies.

"WHO STOLE THE PEOPLE'S MONEY?"—DO TELL .N.Y.TIMES.   'TWAS HIM.

_____ 46. What does the caption tell you about the artist's point of view?

(1) He believes Boss Tweed is a good man.
(2) He believes Boss Tweed has been unfairly accused.
(3) He believes Boss Tweed is guilty.
(4) He believes many people are guilty.

_____ 47. Which of the following is an example of muckraking?

(1) Ida Tarbell's articles about unfair practices in the oil industry
(2) Boss Tweed's control of New York City's police, courts, and newspapers
(3) Mayor Tom Johnson's civic reforms in Cleveland, Ohio
(4) socialists' belief that the government should own and operate a nation's industries

_____ 48. What did the Nineteenth Amendment provide?

(1) It gave women access to higher education.
(2) It allowed women to work outside the home.
(3) It gave women the right to vote.
(4) It prevented women from drinking alcohol.

Base your answer to question 49 on the excerpts below and on your knowledge of social studies.

> **Speaker A:** We declare anew for the entire suppression of the manufacture, sale, importation, exportation, and transportation of alcoholic liquors as a beverage by Federal and State legislation, and the full powers of Government should be exerted to secure this result.

> **Speaker B:** We sympathize with all wise and legitimate efforts to lessen and prevent the evils of intemperance and promote morality.

> **Speaker C:** We are opposed to all sumptuary laws [laws designed to regulate people's habits] as an interference with the individual right of the citizen.

_____ **49.** Which of the speakers supports Prohibition?

    (1) Speaker A
    (2) Speaker C
    (3) Speakers A and B
    (4) Speakers B and C

_____ **50.** Which of the following statements about President Theodore Roosevelt is true?

    (1) He left the Republican Party to form the Progressive Party.
    (2) He believed that government had no place in regulating business.
    (3) He used federal troops against striking coal miners.
    (4) He fought conservation of the nation's natural resources.

_____ **51.** Why did progressive reformers support an income tax?

    (1) They believed it would raise money for conservation.
    (2) They believed it would raise money to improve safety standards in railroads and mines.
    (3) They believed it would lead to lower tariffs, which would lead to lower prices for goods.
    (4) They believed it would lead to more government regulation of banking activities.

_____ **52.** Which is an example of a progressive reform that resulted in discrimination?

    (1) trade union reforms
    (2) the founding of the Tuskegee Institute
    (3) woman suffrage
    (4) the Chinese Exclusion Act

_____ **53.** Which of the following best describes Booker T. Washington?

   (1) He believed that white, male Americans should make decisions for all of society.
   (2) He formed the American Protective Association in 1887.
   (3) He believed that economic power would help African Americans demand equality.
   (4) He believed that farming and industrial skills were unimportant for African Americans.

Base your answer to question 54 on the passage below and on your knowledge of social studies.

"The real purpose of these savage demonstrations is to teach the Negro that in the South he has no rights that the law will enforce. Samuel Hose was burned to teach the Negroes that no matter what a white man does to them, they must not resist. Hose, a servant, had killed Cranford, his employer. An example must be made. Ordinary punishment was deemed inadequate. This Negro must be burned alive. To make the burning a certainty the charge of outrage was invented, and added to the charge of murder. The daily press offered reward for the capture of Hose and then openly incited the people to burn him as soon as caught. The mob carried out the plan in every savage detail."
   —*from* Lynch Law in Georgia *by Ida B. Wells-Barnett, 1899*

_____ **54.** What is Wells's point of view?

   (1) She supports the Southern press.
   (2) She believes that the punishment fits the crime.
   (3) She doesn't think Hose deserved to be punished.
   (4) She is against the actions and the Southern press.

_____ **55.** In the case of *Plessy* v. *Ferguson*, the Supreme Court legalized

   (1) civil rights for African Americans
   (2) segregation
   (3) land ownership by Asian immigrants
   (4) the existence of the Ku Klux Klan

Part II: Constructed-Response Questions

DIRECTIONS: Answer the questions that follow the graph using the space provided. Base your answers to the questions on the graph below and on your knowledge of social studies.

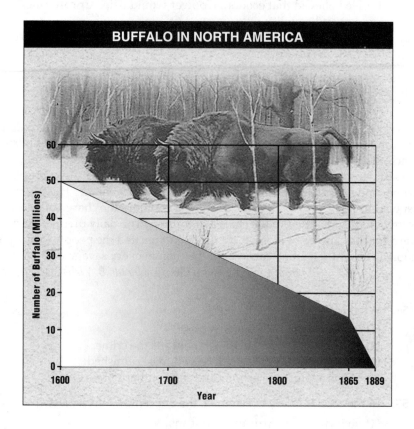

1. According to the graph, during which period did the number of buffalo decrease the most?

   _____

   _____

2. Why did the number of buffalo decrease so sharply during that period?

   _____

   _____

3. In what ways did the ability of the Plains Indians to sustain themselves change after 1889?

   _____

   _____

   _____

DIRECTIONS: *Answer the questions that follow the written document using the space provided. Base your answers to the questions on the reading below and on your knowledge of social studies.*

> ... Sod is the most available material, in fact, the only material the home-steader has at hand, unless he happens to be one of the fortunates who secured a creek claim with timber suitable for house logs. ... At first these sod houses are unplastered, and this is thought perfectly all right, but such a house is somewhat cold in the winter, as the crevices between the sods admit some cold air; so some of the houses are plastered with a kind of "native lime," made of sand and a very sticky native clay. ... The people who live in sod houses, and, in fact, all who live under a dirt roof, are pestered with swarms of bed bugs. ... The vermin were not brought here by the immigrants; they grew on the trees along the river and creeks before the first settlers arrived. The bugs infest the log and sod chicken coops, too, in countless thousands, or, if you wish to measure them in a spoon, you can gather them up in that way from between the sods in the wall. I have heard chicken raisers complain that their fowls are killed by the bugs getting into their ears. Whether or not that is the cause of the fowls dying, the bugs are blamed. Where the sod houses are plastered the bed bugs are not such a nuisance. You don't have to keep a dog in order to have plenty of fleas, for they are natives too and do their best to drive out the intruding settlers. Just have a dirt floor and you have fleas, sure. They seem to spring from the dust of the earth. Coal, oil and water are sometimes used to sprinkle the floor, but that abates the pest only for a short time, and oil costs 35 cents a gallon. People who have board floors are not bothered so much with these fleas.
>
> —*excerpts from the 1870s letters of Howard Ruede, a young pioneer*

1. Why were pioneers forced to use sod for building?

_____

_____

2. What specific problems did sod pose?

_____

_____

3. How does Ruede seem to feel about his pioneer experience? Explain.

_____

_____

_____

Part III: Document-Based Questions

This exercise is designed to test your ability to work with historical documents. It is similar to the document-based questions that you will see on the Intermediate-Level Test in Social Studies. While you are asked to analyze three historical documents, the exercise on the Intermediate-Level Test in Social Studies may include up to nine documents.

Some of the documents have been edited for the purposes of the question. As you analyze the documents, take into account the source of each document and any point of view that may be presented in the document.

Historical Context: In the late 1800s and early 1900s, reform movements strived to improve the quality of life of millions of Americans. Women were increasingly active in these reform movements.

Task: Use information from the documents and your knowledge of social studies to answer the questions that follow each document in Part A. Then use your answers to help you write the essay in Part B, in which you will be asked to:

> • Describe three reform movements of the Progressive Era in which women were involved.
> • Explain two changes in women's lives during that era that might account for their increasing involvement in reform movements.

Part A: Short-Answer Questions

DIRECTIONS: Analyze the documents and answer the questions that follow each document in the space provided. Your answers to the questions will help you write the essay.

Document 1 Educator and newspaper editor Carrie Chapman Catt, speaking to a suffrage association in 1902

> The whole aim of the [women's] movement has been to destroy the idea that obedience is necessary to women; to train women to such self-respect that they would not grant obedience and to train men to such comprehension of equity [fairness] they would not exact [demand] it.

1.a According to Catt, what was the main goal of the women's movement?

_____

_____

  b In Catt's view, what had to be done to prevent men from demanding women's obedience?

_____

_____

Document 2 Florence Kelley, reporting in 1906 on the status of child labor laws to the National Child Labor Committee

> These, I believe, are the gravest obstacles at the present time to the enforce-ment of the child labor law: first, the general hypocrisy of the American people, believing that child labor is an evil, and that, therefore, we do not tolerate it—when there are working children on the streets before our eyes, every working day in the year, in every manufacturing city; second, the failure to make the work of enforcing the law a desirable and recognized profession into which the ablest men will willingly go.

2.a According to Kelley, why are child labor laws not enforced?

_____

_____

_____

  b Why does Kelley think the American people are hypocritical about child labor?

_____

_____

_____

Document 3 Social worker Jane Addams, founder of Chicago's Hull House in 1889, describing the slums of Chicago

> The policy of the public authorities of never taking an initiative, and always waiting to be urged to do their duty, is obviously fatal in a neighborhood where there is little initiative among the citizens. The idea underlying our self-government breaks down in such a ward. The streets are inexpressibly dirty, the number of schools inadequate, sanitary legislation unenforced, the street lighting bad, the paving miserable and altogether lacking in the alleys and smaller streets, and the stables foul beyond description. Hundreds of houses are unconnected with the street sewer.

3. According to Addams, why are the poor and immigrant neighborhoods in such bad condition?

   _____

   _____

Part B: Essay

DIRECTIONS: *Write a well-organized essay that includes an introduction, several paragraphs, and a conclusion. Use evidence from the three documents in the body of the essay. Support your response with relevant facts, examples, and details. Include additional outside information.*

> • Describe three reform movements of the Progressive Era in which women were involved.
> • Explain two changes in women's lives during that era that might account for their increasing involvement in reform movements.

Unit 8—Expansion and War, *1865–1920*

Overview

For years Americans followed a foreign policy of isolationism. Following the Civil War, however, many wanted to expand trade with foreign nations and add territory to an American empire. In April 1898, circumstances led the United States to declare war on Spain. The American military fought in Cuba and the Spanish colony of the Philippines. Within months, the war was over and the United States had acquired more territory.

With a growing empire and trade concerns in Asia, the United States saw the need to build a canal across Central America. By 1914, the Panama Canal was opened to ships. Theodore Roosevelt's "big stick" diplomacy, William Howard Taft's "dollar diplomacy," and Woodrow Wilson's "moral diplomacy" carried on the United States's policy of intervention in foreign countries.

For years events in Europe had been building toward World War I. When Europe went to war in 1914, most Americans believed that the events in Europe would not concern them. Although President Wilson tried to maintain U.S. neutrality, events drew the country toward war. In April 1917, the United States finally declared war on Germany. On the home front, the war affected almost every part of American life. On November 11, 1918, an armistice was signed, but President Wilson's plan for peace—the Fourteen Points—faced opposition at the peace conference and at home.

Essential Questions

As you prepare for the Intermediate-Level Test in Social Studies, ask yourself these essential questions:

- What factors contributed to the growth of American imperialism?

- How did competition for influence in China and the Pacific region lead to new foreign policies?

- What were the causes and results of the Spanish-American War?

- What factors led to World War I and America's involvement in the war?

- Why did many Americans oppose the Treaty of Versailles?

Part I: Multiple-Choice Questions

DIRECTIONS: *Write the number of the answer that best completes the statement or answers the question.*

_____ 1. What was the result of the Gentlemen's Agreement with Japan?

     (1) Japanese immigration to the United States was restricted.
     (2) The Japanese agreed to accept immigrants from the United States.
     (3) Discrimination against Japanese immigrants was ended.
     (4) Japanese immigrants gained the right to vote.

_____ 2. Which of the following contributed to the growth of American imperialism?

     (1) the wish to become one of the world's most powerful countries
     (2) overcrowding in the United States
     (3) an excess of raw materials in the United States
     (4) an attempt to stop Christianity from spreading around the world

_____ 3. Which of the following statements best describes the U.S. purchase of Alaska?

     (1) Many people thought Alaska was worthless and criticized the purchase.
     (2) Alaska was purchased from Canada.
     (3) Alaska was purchased for less than one million dollars.
     (4) Most people were in favor of the purchase because of Alaska's rich resources.

Base your answers to questions 4 and 5 on the time line below and on your knowledge of social studies.

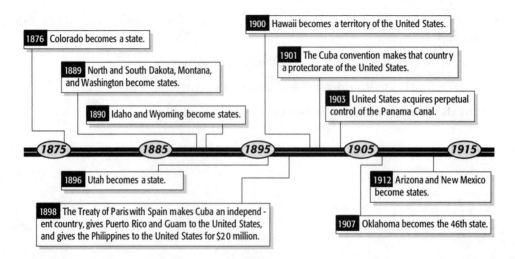

1900 Hawaii becomes a territory of the United States.

1876 Colorado becomes a state.

1901 The Cuba convention makes that country a protectorate of the United States.

1889 North and South Dakota, Montana, and Washington become states.

1903 United States acquires perpetual control of the Panama Canal.

1890 Idaho and Wyoming become states.

1875   1885   1895   1905   1915

1896 Utah becomes a state.

1912 Arizona and New Mexico become states.

1898 The Treaty of Paris with Spain makes Cuba an independent country, gives Puerto Rico and Guam to the United States, and gives the Philippines to the United States for $20 million.

1907 Oklahoma becomes the 46th state.

_____ **4.** In what year were four states added to the union?

    (1) 1876
    (2) 1889
    (3) 1890
    (4) 1896

_____ **5.** With what country did the United States sign the Treaty of Paris?

    (1) Spain
    (2) Cuba
    (3) Japan
    (4) Philippines

_____ **6.** A warning to the nations of Europe not to establish new colonies in the Americas was contained in

    (1) the Pan-American Union
    (2) the Alaska Purchase Treaty
    (3) the Monroe Doctrine
    (4) the Treaty of Kanagawa

_____ **7.** What did Alfred Thayer Mahan say would result from American sea power?

    (1) decreasing American empire
    (2) loss of overseas colonies
    (3) the United States becoming less powerful
    (4) protect shipping and provide access to world markets

_____ **8.** What was the purpose of the John Hay's Open Door policy?

    (1) to resolve the Russo-Japanese War
    (2) to restrict each foreign nation in China to its own sphere of influence
    (3) to encourage the Boxer Rebellion
    (4) to protect and expand American trading interests in China

_____ **9.** Why was the United States interested in the Pacific islands in the 1800s?

    (1) The U.S. wanted to increase immigration from the Pacific islands.
    (2) The islands were important stopping places for ships on their way to Asian nations.
    (3) The United States sought to stop sugar exports.
    (4) The U.S. wanted to improve its relations with Japan.

_____ **10.** Which of the following statements about the U.S. annexation of Hawaii is true?

    (1) American sugar growers opposed annexation.
    (2) President Grover Cleveland supported annexation.
    (3) Most Hawaiians opposed annexation.
    (4) The United States purchased Hawaii from Samoa.

_____ 11. The sensational, biased, and often false news reporting that helped lead to the Spanish-American War is called

(1) yellow journalism
(2) isolationism
(3) armistice
(4) expansionism

_____ 12. Some Americans opposed making the Philippines a possession of the United States because

(1) rule over the Philippines contradicted American principles
(2) the culture of the Philippines was too foreign
(3) they feared it would cause a war to break out in Asia
(4) the Philippines were too far from the mainland United States

_____ 13. A country that is technically independent but actually under the control of another country is called

(1) a monarchy
(2) a protectorate
(3) a democracy
(4) an oligarchy

Base your answer to question 14 on the cartoon below and on your knowledge of social studies.

_____ **14.** What famous Roosevelt saying is represented in this cartoon?

(1) "It is hard to fail, but it is worse never to have tried to succeed."
(2) "There can be no fifty-fifty Americanism in this country."
(3) "Speak softly and carry a big stick."
(4) "We are face to face with our destiny, and we must meet it with a high and resolute courage."

_____ **15.** The isthmus that was chosen as the site for a canal connecting the Atlantic and Pacific Oceans is located in

(1) Colombia
(2) Mexico
(3) Panama
(4) Cuba

_____ **16.** President William Howard Taft's policy of linking American business interests to diplomatic interests was called

(1) moral diplomacy
(2) Roosevelt Corollary
(3) anarchy
(4) dollar diplomacy

_____ **17.** Why did the U.S. help Panama in its struggle for independence from Colombia?

(1) The U.S. wanted to overthrow Colombia.
(2) The U.S. wanted an agreement for the canal with an independent Panama.
(3) The U.S. was appalled by Colombia's treatment of Panamanians.
(4) The U.S. wanted to annex Panama.

_____ **18.** A system that prevents any one country from dominating others is called a

(1) militarism
(2) nationalism
(3) balance of power
(4) dictatorship

_____ **19.** Which incident sparked the beginning of World War I?

(1) the assassination of Archduke Franz Ferdinand of Austria-Hungary
(2) a German invasion of Austria-Hungary
(3) the forming of an alliance between Russia and Serbia
(4) the forming of an alliance between Great Britain and Belgium

Base your answer to question 20 on the map below and on your knowledge of social studies.

NATIONAL GEOGRAPHIC   **EUROPE IN WORLD WAR I, 1914**

Allies
Central Powers
Neutral nations

_____ **20.** What nations made up the Central Powers?

(1) Spain, Portugal, and Italy
(2) Germany, Austria-Hungary, Bulgaria, and the Ottoman Empire
(3) Russia and the Ottoman Empire
(4) Germany, Austria-Hungary, and Romania

_____ **21.** What did both sides realize after the Battle of the Marne?

(1) that trench warfare is a quick way to win a battle
(2) that neither side had the ability to win the war quickly or easily
(3) that armored tanks were not very effective
(4) that they should end the war and form an alliance

_____ 22. Which of the following events contributed to the United States' decision to enter World War I?

(1) Mexicans migrating to the United States
(2) the publication of the Zimmerman telegram
(3) President Woodrow Wilson's call for neutrality
(4) the overthrow of the monarchy in Russia

_____ 23. Information that is designed to influence opinion is called

(1) propaganda
(2) militarism
(3) autocracy
(4) telegram

_____ 24. How did the war in Europe affect the United States financially?

(1) It caused the economy to fail.
(2) It caused Americans to save their money.
(3) It caused banks to close.
(4) It greatly improved the U.S. economy.

_____ 25. One reason that the Allies needed the help of American forces was that

(1) Great Britain withdrew from the war
(2) the Allies were running out of war supplies and food
(3) they had lost the Battle of Argonne Forest
(4) Russia had switched sides

_____ 26. Which of the following was a term of President Wilson's armistice to end World War I?

(1) Germany must accept full responsibility for the war.
(2) The Central Powers were required to evacuate France, Belgium, and Russia.
(3) Russia must accept full responsibility for the war.
(4) The U.S. must pay reparations for war damages.

_____ 27. The gathering of resources and preparation for war is called

(1) espionage
(2) rationing
(3) mobilization
(4) militarism

_____ 28. Where did the United States get most of the money it needed to finance the war?

(1) by borrowing money from Great Britain and France
(2) by encouraging people to buy and eat more food
(3) by fining those who opposed the war
(4) by selling war bonds to the American people

_____ **29.** During World War I, the United States faced

(1) a food shortage
(2) a labor shortage
(3) an electricity shortage
(4) a steel shortage

_____ **30.** Which of the following made it a crime to say, print, or write almost anything perceived as negative about the U.S. government?

(1) the Espionage Act
(2) the Pacifist Act
(3) the Sedition Act and the Sabotage Act
(4) the Liberty Act

Base your answer to question 31 on the outline below and on your knowledge of social studies.

I. Effects of World War I
   A. Destruction in Europe
   B. Boom in the American economy
   C. Allied victory
   D. _____

_____ **31.** Which of the following best completes the outline above?

(1) Nationalist pride
(2) Military buildup
(3) Tangled web of alliances
(4) Defeated empires lose their colonies

_____ **32.** Which term describes a people's right to decide how to be governed?

(1) monarchy
(2) national self-determination
(3) pacifism
(4) socialism

_____ **33.** President Woodrow Wilson's plan for peace after World War I was outlined in a proposal known as

(1) the Fourteen Points
(2) the League of Nations
(3) the Great Migration
(4) the Triple Entente

_____ **34.** President Wilson's proposal to create a League of Nations was

(1) largely supported and accepted
(2) opposed by some and ultimately rejected
(3) first rejected but then changed and accepted
(4) supported by the U.S. but rejected by foreign nations

Part II: Constructed-Response Questions

DIRECTIONS: Read the paragraph below. Then answer the questions based on the reading and on your knowledge of social studies.

> . . . The white race deems itself to be the dominant race in this country. . . . But in view of the Constitution, in the eye of the law, there is in this country no superior, dominant, ruling class of citizens. There is no caste here. Our Constitution is color-blind, and neither knows nor tolerates classes among citizens. In respect of civil rights, all citizens are equal before the law. . . . It is, therefore, to be regretted that this high tribunal, the final expositor of the fundamental law of the land, has reached the conclusion that it is competent for a State to regulate the enjoyment by citizens of their civil rights solely upon the basis of race.
>
> —*U.S. Supreme Court Justice John Harlan writing about the 1896 Supreme Court decision in* Plessy v. Ferguson *that legalized segregation*

1. What does Harlan mean when he writes that the Constitution is color-blind?

   _____

   _____

   _____

   _____

2. According to Harlan, how does the view of the white race differ from the view of the Constitution?

   _____

   _____

   _____

DIRECTIONS: *Read the paragraph below. Then answer the questions based on the reading and on your knowledge of social studies.*

> I walked the floor of the White House night after night until midnight; and I am not ashamed to tell you, gentlemen, that I went down on my knees and prayed Almighty God for light and guidance more than one night. And one night late it came to me this way—I don't know how it was, but it came: (1) That we could not give them back to Spain—that would be cowardly and dishonorable; (2) that we could not turn them over to France, or Germany—our commercial rivals in the Orient—that would be bad business and discreditable; (3) that we could not leave them to themselves—they were unfit for self-government—and they would soon have anarchy and misrule over there worse than Spain's was; and (4) that there was nothing left for us to do but to take them all, and to educate the Filipinos, and uplift and civilize and Christianize them, and by God's grace do the very best we could by them, as our fellow-men for whom Christ also died. And then I went to bed, and went to sleep, and slept soundly, and the next morning I sent for the chief engineer of the War Department (our map-maker), and I told him to put the Philippines on the map of the United States [pointing to a large map on the wall of his office], and there they are, and there they will stay while I am President!
>   —*President William McKinley relating in 1899 his decision to annex the Philippines*

1. Why do you think President McKinley's decision to annex the Philippines was a difficult one?

   _____

   _____

   _____

2. Explain three reasons behind McKinley's decision to annex the Philippines.

   _____

   _____

   _____

3. Why did McKinley think it would have been bad business to give the Philippines to France or Germany?

   _____

   _____

   _____

Part III: Document-Based Questions

This exercise is designed to test your ability to work with historical documents. It is similar to the document-based question that you will see on the Intermediate-Level Test in Social Studies. While you are asked to analyze three historical documents, the exercise on the Intermediate-Level Test in Social Studies may include up to nine documents.

Some of the documents have been edited for the purposes of the question. As you analyze the documents, take into account the source of each document and any point of view that may be presented in the document.

Historical Context: Innovations in technology and new business combinations helped the United States develop into a great industrial power. By the year 1900, United States industrial production was the greatest in the world. This rapid growth had both positive and negative results.

Task: Use information from the documents and your knowledge of social studies to answer the questions that follow each document in Part A. Then use your answers to help you write the essay in Part B in which you will be asked to:

> Discuss the positive and negative social and economic effects of the rapid growth of the United States during the late 1800s.

Part A: Short-Answer Questions

DIRECTIONS: Analyze the documents and answer the short-answer questions that follow.

Document 1 The western-bound Union Pacific and the eastern-bound Central Pacific rail lines came together on May 10, 1869, at Promontory Point, Utah. An onlooker, Alexander Toponce, described the final spike-driving ceremony.

> It was a great occasion, every one carried off souvenirs and there are enough splinters of the last tie in museums to make a good bonfire. When the connection was finally made the Union Pacific and the Central Pacific engineers ran their engines up until their pilots touched. Then the engineers shook hands and had their pictures taken and each broke a bottle of champagne on the pilot of the other's engine and had their picture taken again. The Union Pacific engine, the "Jupiter," was driven by my good friend, George Lashus, who still lives in Ogden. Both before and after the spike driving ceremony there were speeches, which were cheered heartily. I do not remember what any of the speakers said now, but I do remember that there was a great abundance of champagne.

1.*a*   What was the mood during the celebration?

_____

_____

  b   What was the significance of the completion of the Transcontinental Railroad for American business?

_____

_____

  c   How did the growth of the railroads contribute to the growth of the United States' economy?

_____

_____

Document 2   Life in the sweatshops is described in these excerpts from an 1893 report by the Illinois Bureau of Labor Statistics.

> . . . A few examples may be cited illustrating what some of these places are like. In one case, several men were found at work pressing knee pants in a low basement room, poorly lighted and ventilated by two small windows. . . . In another case, seven persons were at work in a room 12 by 15 feet in dimensions and with but two windows. . . . Charcoal was used for heating the pressers' irons, and the air was offensive and prostrating to a degree. . . .
>
> Very few sweaters' victims accumulate any savings. When they do they become sweaters themselves. . . . [T]hey manifest great desire to see their children attain some degree of prosperity greater than their own. Unfortunately, their eagerness in this particular frequently defeats itself, for they send their young children to the shop instead of to the school. Here their health is undermined; their presence in the shop reduces the wages of adults, and both parents and children become involved in a common struggle for existence. . . .

2.*a* What is the difference between the "sweaters" and the "sweaters' victims"?

_____

_____

b What long-term problem is caused by children working instead of going to school?

_____

_____

_____

Document 3 Andrew Carnegie published an article called "Wealth," excerpts of which appear here. (1889)

> . . . One who studies this subject will soon be brought face to face with the conclusion that upon the sacredness of property civilization itself depends—the right of the laborer to his $100 in the savings bank, and equally the legal right of the millionaire to his millions. . . .
>
> There are but three modes in which surplus wealth can be disposed of. It can be left to the families of the decedents; or it can be bequeathed for public purposes; or, finally, it can be administered during their lives by its possessors. . . . In bestowing charity, the main consideration should be to help those who will help themselves; to provide part of the means by which those who desire to improve may do so; to give those who desire to rise the aids by which they may rise; to assist, but rarely or never to do all. Neither the individual nor the race is improved by almsgiving. . . .
>
> Thus is the problem of rich and poor to be solved. The laws of accumulation will be left free; the laws of distribution free. Individualism will continue, but the millionaire will be but a trustee for the poor; entrusted for a season with a great part of the increased wealth of the community, but administering it for the community far better than it could or would have done for itself.

3.*a* On what does Carnegie think that civilization depends?

_____

b What does Carnegie think wealthy people should do with their wealth?

_____

_____

_____

c Who does Carnegie think should be the recipients?

_____

_____

_____

Part B: Essay

DIRECTIONS: *Write a well-organized essay that includes an introduction, several paragraphs, and a conclusion. Use evidence from the documents in the body of the essay. Support your response with relevant facts, examples, and details. Include additional outside information.*

> Discuss the positive and negative social and economic effects of the rapid growth of the United States during the late 1800s.

Unit 9—Turbulent Decades, *1919–1939*

Overview

As World War I ended, Americans wanted to withdraw from world affairs. A "Red Scare" increased Americans' distrust of many foreigners. Warren G. Harding was elected president in 1920, but scandal and corruption marred his administration. Harding's successor, Calvin Coolidge, took an active role in supporting business, and the economy boomed. The temperance movement achieved its goal in 1920 with the Eighteenth Amendment—a prohibition on the manufacture, sale, and transportation of liquor. Changes in the 1920s affected every aspect of American life.

The nation's economic prosperity in the 1920s led Americans to invest heavily in the stock market. By October 1929, stock prices dropped drastically as investors sold millions of shares and the United States slid into the Great Depression. President Franklin Roosevelt and Congress passed a program called the New Deal to help the economic problems of the Depression. The southern Great Plains suffered a severe drought during this time. The region became known as the Dust Bowl, and farmers there went bankrupt. The effects of the Great Depression were also felt throughout Europe.

Essential Questions

As you prepare for the Intermediate-Level Test in Social Studies, ask yourself these essential questions:

- How did the prosperity of the 1920s affect the nation and its people?
- What caused the stock market crash?
- How did President Hoover react to the Great Depression?
- How did President Roosevelt restore the confidence of the American people?

Part I: Multiple-Choice Questions

DIRECTIONS: *Write the number of the answer that best completes the statement or answers the question.*

_____ 1. American intolerance in the 1920s was shown by

(1) the rejection of jazz   (3) the support of labor unions
(2) a distrust of foreigners   (4) racial unity and pride

_____ 2. Why did membership in unions drop during the 1920s?

(1) People associated unions with immigrants.
(2) People associated unions with radicals.
(3) People associated unions with rising debt.
(4) People associated unions with racial unrest.

_____ 3. Marcus Garvey is best known for his support of

(1) integration
(2) the Russian Revolution
(3) the back-to-Africa movement
(4) the Red Scare

_____ 4. One method used by the U.S. government in the 1920s to promote American business was

(1) increased government spending
(2) higher income taxes
(3) higher wages for women and children
(4) higher protective tariffs

Base your answer to question 5 on the outline below and on your knowledge of social studies.

I. Organized labor's reasons for better wages

A. Rapidly rising prices
B. Rising debt
C. _____

_____ 5. Which of the following would best complete the outline above?

(1) Longer work week
(2) Fewer women employed
(3) Fear of immigrants
(4) Wages unchanged since wartime

_____ 6. The Teapot Dome scandal became a symbol of

(1) government corruption
(2) a return to normalcy
(3) racial unrest
(4) isolationism

_____ 7. Which of the following statements best describes the Kellogg-Briand Pact?

(1) It was successful in enforcing peace.
(2) It called for outlawing war.
(3) It called for an end to government corruption.
(4) It brought an end to the Boston police strike.

Base your answer to question 8 on the passage and list below and on your knowledge of social studies.

By 1927, 4 out of 5 cars had closed tops, compared with only 1 in 10 in 1919. Now protected from the weather, many families hopped into their cars for short day trips. Many city workers moved to houses in the new suburbs. Car owners now traveled easily to once-distant places, bringing far-flung Americans together for the first time.

Generalizations About the Automobile
A. Automobiles were too expensive to buy.
B. The automobile changed American culture in many ways.
C. Many businesses arose from the need to service the newly mobile nation.
D. Suburbs grew as a result of the automobile.

————— 8. Which of the generalizations above are supported by the details in this passage?
(1) A and B   (3) B and D
(2) B and C   (4) C and D

————— 9. Which of the following benefited from the auto industry in the 1920s?
(1) the tourism industry   (3) the Harlem Renaissance
(2) air quality   (4) Charles Lindbergh

————— 10. Which of the following contributed to a strong economy in the 1920s?
(1) installment buying
(2) slow industrial growth
(3) a decrease in consumer demand for products
(4) the computer industry

Base your answer to question 11 on the poem excerpt below and on your knowledge of social studies.

Well, son, I'll tell you:
Life for me ain't been no crystal stair.
It's had tacks in it,
And splinters,
And boards torn up,
And places with no carpet on the floor–
—*from* Mother to Son *by Langston Hughes*

————— 11. What is the message of the excerpt?
(1) Life has been difficult for the speaker.
(2) Life has been easy for the speaker.
(3) Thinking about the past is painful for the speaker.
(4) The speaker has not lived in a nice house all her life.

Base your answer to question 12 on the time line below and on your knowledge of social studies.

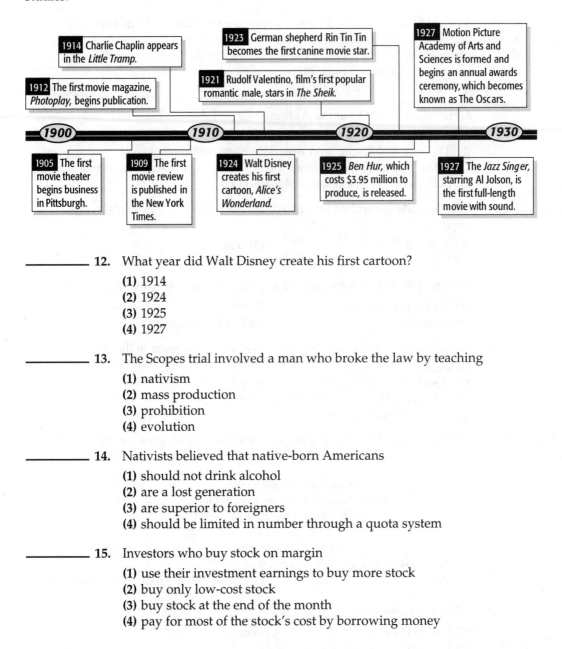

1914 Charlie Chaplin appears in the *Little Tramp.*

1912 The first movie magazine, *Photoplay,* begins publication.

1923 German shepherd Rin Tin Tin becomes the first canine movie star.

1921 Rudolf Valentino, film's first popular romantic male, stars in *The Sheik.*

1927 Motion Picture Academy of Arts and Sciences is formed and begins an annual awards ceremony, which becomes known as The Oscars.

1900   **1910**   **1920**   **1930**

1905 The first movie theater begins business in Pittsburgh.

1909 The first movie review is published in the New York Times.

1924 Walt Disney creates his first cartoon, *Alice's Wonderland.*

1925 *Ben Hur,* which costs $3.95 million to produce, is released.

1927 The *Jazz Singer,* starring Al Jolson, is the first full-length movie with sound.

_____ **12.** What year did Walt Disney create his first cartoon?

     (1) 1914
     (2) 1924
     (3) 1925
     (4) 1927

_____ **13.** The Scopes trial involved a man who broke the law by teaching

     (1) nativism
     (2) mass production
     (3) prohibition
     (4) evolution

_____ **14.** Nativists believed that native-born Americans

     (1) should not drink alcohol
     (2) are a lost generation
     (3) are superior to foreigners
     (4) should be limited in number through a quota system

_____ **15.** Investors who buy stock on margin

     (1) use their investment earnings to buy more stock
     (2) buy only low-cost stock
     (3) buy stock at the end of the month
     (4) pay for most of the stock's cost by borrowing money

_____ **16.** Why were shantytowns for the homeless sometimes called "Hoovervilles"?

     (1) They were constructed in President Herbert Hoover's hometown.
     (2) President Herbert Hoover ordered their construction.
     (3) They were symbolic of President Herbert Hoover's failure to help victims of the Depression.
     (4) The name honored President Herbert Hoover for his efforts to fight homelessness.

_____ **17.** One factor that led to the Great Depression was

     (1) heavy rains in the Great Plains
     (2) too many public works projects
     (3) the stock market crash
     (4) buying goods with cash

Base your answer to question 18 on the graph below and on your knowledge of social studies.

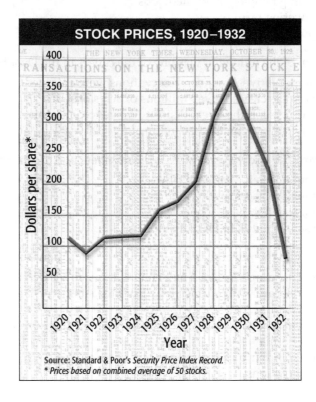

STOCK PRICES, 1920–1932

Source: Standard & Poor's *Security Price Index Record.*
* Prices based on combined average of 50 stocks.

_____ **18.** During what years was the average stock price over $200 per share?

     (1) 1925–1930   **(3)** 1927–1931
     (2) 1926–1932   **(4)** 1928–1931

_____ **19.** President Franklin D. Roosevelt's overall plan for improving the nation's economy was called

(1) the New Deal
(2) the Tennessee Valley Authority
(3) fireside chats
(4) the Bonus Army

_____ **20.** What effect did Roosevelt's radio talks have on the American people?

(1) He gained the support and confidence of the American public.
(2) They had no effect on the American people.
(3) People were panicked by them.
(4) The American people ignored the radio talks.

_____ **21.** Roosevelt's New Deal programs gave high priority to

(1) flood control
(2) giving people government jobs
(3) lowering farm prices
(4) punishing the banks

_____ **22.** Which of the following was one of the causes of the Dust Bowl?

(1) Some Native American reservations were enlarged.
(2) Farmers cleared away millions of acres of sod.
(3) Farmers left the Great Plains to move to California.
(4) Fascism was on the rise in Europe.

_____ **23.** During the Great Depression, large numbers of African Americans

(1) found jobs in Southern cities
(2) found jobs on Southern farms
(3) migrated to Northern cities
(4) established their own businesses

_____ **24.** What was the purpose of the Indian Reorganization Act of 1934?

(1) to encourage Native Americans to move to Mexico
(2) to relocate Native Americans from the southern states to the northern states
(3) to encourage Native Americans to become migrant workers in California
(4) to restore tribal government and provide money to enlarge some reservations

Base your answer to question 25 on the cartoon below and on your knowledge of social studies.

_____ **25.** What does the cartoonist believe the new president, Franklin D. Roosevelt, will do when he takes office?

    (1) Roosevelt will clean up corruption in the Democratic Party.

    (2) He will let Congress run the country without interference.

    (3) He will clean up state governments.

    (4) He will bring new ideas to the federal government with the help of the Congress.

_____ **26.** The Social Security Act of 1935 launched

    (1) a national labor union

    (2) agricultural reform

    (3) a national welfare system

    (4) the Roosevelt Recession

_____ **27.** Why was Roosevelt's plan to change the Supreme Court criticized?

    (1) Critics didn't want the court to agree with Roosevelt.

    (2) Critics didn't like the system of checks and balances.

    (3) Critics didn't want to add to the number of justices.

    (4) Critics thought he was trying to pack the court with justices who would agree with him.

_____ **28.** Senator Huey Long's "Share Our Wealth Plan" called for

  (1) heavily taxing the rich and distributing the tax money to the
    financially needy
  (2) giving big businesses a tax break
  (3) abolishing prisoner rehab programs
  (4) ending unemployment insurance

Part II: Constructed-Response Questions

DIRECTIONS: *Analyze the graph below. Then answer the questions based on the graph and on your knowledge of social studies.*

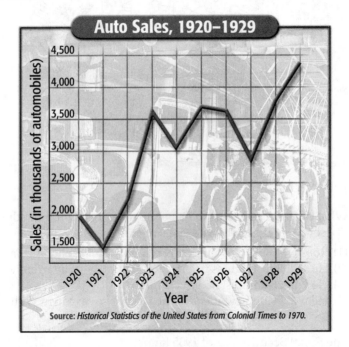

Source: *Historical Statistics of the United States from Colonial Times to 1970.*

1. About how many fewer autos were sold in 1921 than in 1920?

_____

_____

_____

2. Between which two consecutive years did auto sales rise the most?

_____

_____

_____

3. Looking at the trend in auto sales overall for the 1920s, what generalization could you make about consumers in the 1920s?

_____

_____

_____

DIRECTIONS: *Analyze the graph below. Then answer the questions based on the graph and on your knowledge of social studies.*

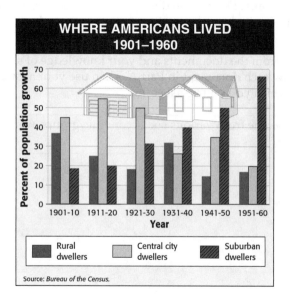

WHERE AMERICANS LIVED
1901–1960

Rural dwellers

Central city dwellers

Suburban dwellers

Source: *Bureau of the Census.*

1. Between 1920 and 1940, what percentage of population growth was in the central cities?

_____

_____

2. How did the percentage of suburban dwellers change from 1920 to 1940?

_____

_____

3. Which group experienced increases in percent of population growth between 1920 and 1930?

_____

_____

Part III: Document-Based Questions

This exercise is designed to test your ability to work with historical documents. It is similar to the document-based questions that you will see on the Intermediate-Level Test in Social Studies. While you are asked to analyze three historical documents, the exercise on the Intermediate-Level Test in Social Studies may include up to nine documents.

Some of the documents have been edited for the purposes of the question. As you analyze the documents, take into account the source of each document and any point of view that may be presented in the document.

Historical Context: The Great Depression deeply affected Americans' lives. Not every worker lost a job, and not every family lost a home. But most Americans had to make do with less income, less food, and less security.

Task: Use information from the documents and your knowledge of social studies to answer the questions that follow each document in Part A. Then use your answers to help you write the essay in Part B, in which you will be asked to:

> Describe how people from various socioeconomic groups were affected by the Depression.

Part A: Short-Answer Questions

DIRECTIONS: *Analyze the documents and answer the questions that follow each document in the space provided. Your answers to the questions will help you write the essay.*

Document 1 Frederick Lewis Allen writing about the Depression in his book *Since Yesterday*

> But if you knew where to look, some of them [signs of the Depression] would begin to appear. First, the breadlines in the poorer districts. Second, those bleak settlements ironically known as "Hoovervilles" in the outskirts of the cities and on vacant lots—groups of makeshift shacks constructed out of packing boxes, scrap iron, anything that could be picked up free in a diligent combing of the city dumps: shacks in which men and sometimes whole families of evicted people were sleeping on automobile seats carried from auto-graveyards, warming themselves before fires of rubbish in grease drums. Third, the homeless people sleeping in doorways or on park benches, and going the rounds of the restaurants for leftover half-eaten biscuits, piecrusts, anything to keep the fires of life burning. . . . Among the comparatively well-to-do people of the country (those, let us say, whose pre-depression incomes had been over $5,000 a year) the great majority were living on a reduced scale, for salary cuts had been extensive, especially since 1931, and dividends were dwindling. These people were discharging servants, or cutting servants' wages to a minimum, or in some cases "letting" a servant stay on without other compensation than board and lodging. . . . Alongside these men and women of the well-to-do classes whose fortunes had been merely reduced by the depression were others whose fortunes had been shattered. The crowd of men waiting for the 8:14 train at the prosperous suburb included many who had lost their jobs, and were going to town as usual not merely to look stubbornly and almost hopelessly for other work but also to keep up a bold front of activity. . . . There were architects and engineers bound for offices to which no clients had come in weeks. There were doctors who thought themselves lucky when a patient paid a bill.

1.*a* What three socioeconomic classes does the author describe in the document?

_____

_____

　b Why do you think some jobless men would go to town to "keep up a bold front of activity"?

_____

_____

Document 2 Malcolm Cowley writing about the 1932 U.S. Army attack on the Bonus Army camp of World War I veterans

> Their shanties and tents had been burned, their personal property destroyed, except for the few belongings they could carry on their backs; many of their families were separated, wives from husbands, children from parents. Knowing all this, they still did not appreciate the extent of their losses. Two days before, they had regarded themselves, and thought the country regarded them, as heroes trying to collect a debt long overdue. They had boasted about their months or years of service, their medals, their wounds, their patriotism in driving the Reds out of their camp; they had nailed an American flag to every hut. When threatened with forcible eviction, they answered that no American soldier would touch them: hadn't a detachment of Marines . . . thrown down its arms and refused to march against them? But the infantry, last night, had driven them out like so many vermin. Mr. Hoover [President Herbert Hoover] . . . and his subordinates, in their eagerness to justify his action, were about to claim that the veterans were Red radicals, that they were the dregs of the population, that most of them had criminal records and, as a final insult, that half of them weren't veterans at all.

2.*a* According to the document, why did the veterans believe they were owed payment on a long overdue debt?

_____

_____

  b According to the document, how did President Hoover justify the attack on the veterans?

_____

_____

Document 3 John Steinbeck writing about migrant farm workers escaping the Dust Bowl in his novel *The Grapes of Wrath*

> And as the families moved westward, the technique of building up a home in the evening and tearing it down with the morning light became fixed; so that the folded tent was packed in one place, the cooking pots counted in their box. And as the cars moved westward, each member of the family grew into his proper place, grew into his duties; so that each member, old and young, had his place in the car; so that in the weary, hot evenings, when the cars pulled into the camping places, each member had his duty and went to it without instruction: children to gather wood, to carry water; men to pitch tents and bring down the beds; women to cook the supper and to watch while the family fed. . . . The families, which had been units of which the boundaries were a house at night, a farm by day, changed their boundaries. . . . They were not farm men any more, but migrant men. And the thought, the planning, the long staring silence that had gone out to the fields, went now to the roads, to the distance, to the West. That man whose mind had been bound with acres lived with narrow concrete miles. And his thought and his worry were not any more with rainfall, with wind and dust, with the thrust of the crops. Eyes watched the tires, ears listened to the clattering motors, and minds struggled with oil, with gasoline, with the thinning rubber between air and road. Then a broken gear was tragedy. Then water in the evening was the yearning, and food over the fire. . . . The wills thrust westward ahead of them, and fears that had once apprehended drought or flood now lingered with anything that might stop the westward crawling.

3. According to the document, how did the goals and daily problems of the farmers change when they became migrants?

_____

_____

Part B: Essay

DIRECTIONS: *Write a well-organized essay that includes an introduction, several paragraphs, and a conclusion. Use evidence from the three documents in the body of the essay. Support your response with relevant facts, examples, and details. Include additional outside information.*

> Describe how people from various socioeconomic groups were affected by the Depression.

Unit 10—The Role of the United States in the World, *1939–1990*

Overview

As the United States dealt with the Great Depression, Germany and Italy struggled with the effects of World War I. Benito Mussolini established a fascist dictatorship in Italy, while Adolf Hitler and his Nazi Party established a totalitarian state in Germany. In 1939, Hitler sent his German armies into Poland. When Britain and France declared war on Germany, World War II began. When Japan attacked the American military base at Pearl Harbor, Hawaii, on December 7, 1941, the United States entered the war. After years of battle in Europe and North Africa, Germany surrendered unconditionally on May 7, 1945. As the Allies moved across Europe, they discovered the horror of the Holocaust. After the United States dropped an atomic bomb on Hiroshima, and then a second bomb on Nagasaki, the Japanese government agreed to surrender. World War II was finally over.

After World War II, the Soviet Union began to set up communist governments. A growing distrust developed between the Soviet Union and the Western nations. The United States adopted a policy of containment to contain the spread of communism. In June 1950 North Korea invaded South Korea. The president asked the United Nations to send forces to defend the South Koreans. After two years of fighting a cease-fire was finally reached. Neither side achieved victory or gained much territory.

The Eisenhower years saw a rise in prosperity for many Americans. The Cold War also affected events in the 1950s. Defense spending increased and the nuclear arms race continued.

In Southeast Asia, a conflict that began after World War II grew steadily worse. Thousands of American troops were sent to Vietnam to stem the spread of communism. 1968 was a year of tragedies for the United States. While thousands of Americans were killed in Vietnam, Martin Luther King, Jr., and presidential candidate Robert Kennedy were assassinated. Over the next few years, President Nixon pulled American troops out of Vietnam. South Vietnam fell to the Communists, but in 1975 the long war was over.

President Nixon hoped to ease tensions in the world and create a greater opportunity for peace. He did this by opening diplomatic relations with Communist China and signing a Strategic Arms Limitation Treaty with the Soviet Union. A crisis soon arose for Nixon, however, when war broke out in the Middle East in 1973.

In 1976, Americans turned to Jimmy Carter to lead them. In November 1979, a group of Iranian students took 52 Americans hostage. This crisis and the inability of the administration to negotiate the hostages' release led Americans to vote for Ronald Reagan in 1980. Ronald Reagan's presidency marked a significant conservative shift in America. His successor, George H.W. Bush, was an experienced leader in foreign affairs. His presidency saw the end of communism in the Soviet Union as well as the end of the Soviet Union.

In 1990, Iraq invaded neighboring Kuwait. President Bush persuaded other nations to join in Operation Desert Storm. The allies succeeded in forcing Iraqi troops to pull out of Kuwait. Another challenge to world peace arose in Yugoslavia. The United Nations sent in peacekeeping teams to prevent the Serbs from committing further atrocities.

Essential Questions

As you prepare for the Intermediate-Level Test in Social Studies, ask yourself these essential questions:

- What events led to World War II in Europe?
- Why did the United States enter the war?
- How did World War II affect Americans at home?
- What role did the atomic bomb play in ending the war?
- What was the Holocaust?
- How did the United States attempt to stop the spread of communism in the 1950s and 1960s?
- What events led to the Korean War?
- What effect did Cold War fears have on domestic politics?
- What events led to America's involvement in, and withdrawal from, Vietnam?
- How did the Vietnam War affect life at home?
- How did Richard Nixon change U.S. political relations with the Soviet Union and China?
- How did President Carter bring temporary peace to the Middle East?
- What changes took place in the Soviet Union in the 1980s?

Part I: Multiple-Choice Questions

DIRECTIONS: *Write the number of the answer that best completes the statement or answers the question.*

_____ 1. Which set of events is in the correct chronological order?
   (1) the United States joins World War II — the stock market crashes — the Great Depression begins
   (2) the Great Depression begins — the United States joins World War II — the stock market crashes
   (3) the stock market crashes — the Great Depression begins — the United States joins World War II
   (4) the Great Depression begins — the stock market crashes — the United States joins World War II

_____ 2. One factor that contributed to Adolf Hitler's rise in popularity among Germans was

   (1) an economic boom in Germany
   (2) his support of the Treaty of Versailles
   (3) his great skill as a public speaker
   (4) the Works Progress Administration

_____ 3. The Neutrality Acts aimed to

   (1) stop Joseph Stalin's rise to power in the Soviet Union
   (2) keep the United States out of wars
   (3) establish a totalitarian state
   (4) join Japan, Germany, and Italy in an alliance

_____ 4. What goals did the leaders of Germany, Italy, and Japan share in the 1930s?

   (1) to expand their political power and add to their nation's territory
   (2) to become more powerful than the others
   (3) to establish totalitarian states and have complete power over the citizens of each nation
   (4) to establish work camps to imprison political opponents

_____ 5. A political system based on extreme nationalism and racism is called

   (1) appeasement   **(3)** fascism
   (2) capitalism   **(4)** blitzkrieg

_____ 6. The Axis Powers in World War II consisted of

   (1) Germany, Italy, and Japan
   (2) Germany, the Soviet Union, and Poland
   (3) Italy, Japan, and China
   (4) Great Britain, the United States, and the Soviet Union

_____ 7. The Lend-Lease Act of 1941 allowed the United States to

   (1) join the British in the Battle of Britain
   (2) stop Japan from seizing Indochina
   (3) support the Allied countries by selling, lending, or leasing arms and other war supplies to them
   (4) stop Germany from invading the Soviet Union

_____ 8. What incident finally forced the United States to join World War II?

   (1) the executions ordered by Joseph Stalin
   (2) the signing of the Atlantic Charter
   (3) the German invasion of Poland
   (4) the Japanese attack on the U.S. military base in Pearl Harbor, Hawaii

Base your answer to question 9 on the quotation below and on your knowledge of social studies.

> "In the Navy housing areas around Pearl Harbor, people couldn't imagine what was wrecking Sunday morning. Captain Reynolds Hayden, enjoying breakfast at his home on Hospital Point, thought it was construction blasting . . . Lieutenant C. E. Boudreau, drying down after a shower, thought an oil tank had blown up near his quarters . . . until a Japanese plane almost grazed the bathroom window."

_____ 9. What key tactic of the Japanese attack on Pearl Harbor is illustrated in the passage?

(1) thoughtlessness

(2) surprise

(3) vulnerability

(4) excitability

_____ 10. Some Americans questioned how loyal Japanese Americans would be if Japan invaded the United States. Because of this, the U.S. government

(1) tried to earn Japanese Americans' loyalty by giving them tax breaks

(2) relocated Japanese Americans to Greenland

(3) relocated many Japanese Americans into detention centers called internment camps

(4) trained Japanese Americans to attack the Japanese

_____ 11. What was one reason for the shortage of consumer goods in the United States during World War II?

(1) Factories that made consumer goods were converted to make military equipment.

(2) Most consumers were men, and many men had left the country to fight in the war.

(3) Most consumer goods were sent overseas.

(4) Racial violence in cities slowed down factory production.

Base your answers to questions 12 and 13 on the line graph below and on your knowledge of social studies.

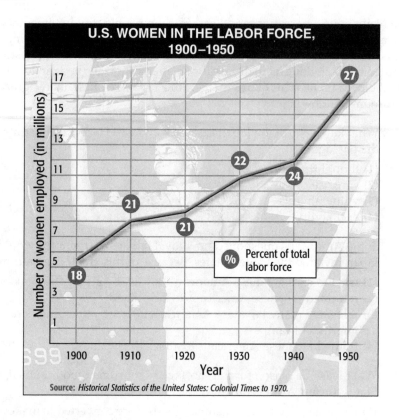

U.S. WOMEN IN THE LABOR FORCE, 1900–1950

Source: *Historical Statistics of the United States: Colonial Times to 1970.*

_____ **12.** In 1940, what percent of the labor force was made up of women?
   (1) 21
   (2) 22
   (3) 24
   (4) 27

_____ **13.** Why did the percentage of women in the workforce rise so dramatically from 1940 to 1950?
   (1) They were cheaper to hire than men.
   (2) Many men were joining the armed forces.
   (3) The government hired many women.
   (4) Men encouraged their wives to work.

_____ **14.** On D-Day, Allied forces landed on the shores of
   (1) Moscow   **(3)** Sicily
   (2) Paris   **(4)** Normandy

_____ **15.** What was the Nazis' "final solution of the Jewish question"?

    (1) driving Jewish people out of Germany by raising their taxes

    (2) forcing Jewish people to fight in the Battle of the Bulge

    (3) killing all the Jewish people in Europe

    (4) relocating Jewish people to the Soviet Union

Base your answer to question 16 on the map below and on your knowledge of social studies.

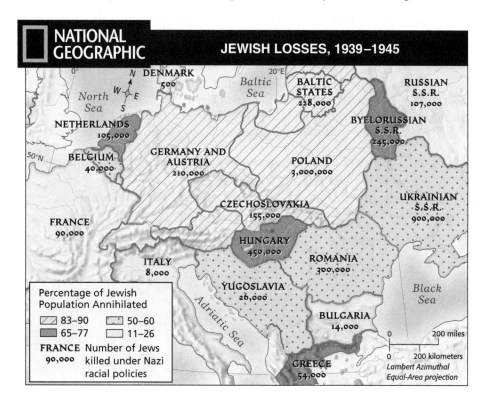

_____ **16.** What country had the highest number of Jews in its population killed?

    (1) Greece

    (2) France

    (3) Hungary

    (4) Poland

_____ **17.** What took place in the Japanese city of Hiroshima on August 6, 1945?

    (1) The Japanese forces defeated the Allied forces.

    (2) The United States dropped an atomic bomb on the city, causing immense destruction, injury, and death.

    (3) The Allies issued the Potsdam Declaration.

    (4) Japan signed the formal surrender.

_____ **18.** After the war ended, who was put on trial in the Nuremberg trials?

   (1) top German and Japanese leaders   **(3)** Benito Mussolini
   (2) Joseph Stalin   **(4)** kamikaze pilots

_____ **19.** At the 1945 Yalta conference, control of Germany was divided among

   (1) Japan, France, the United States, and Britain
   (2) France, the Soviet Union, Britain, and Italy
   (3) the Soviet Union, the United States, Britain, and France
   (4) France, Italy, Britain, and Japan

_____ **20.** The United Nations was intended to be

   (1) a group of nations joined to fight the Soviet Union
   (2) a group of nations in control of Germany
   (3) a group of nations joined to fight the spread of communism
   (4) an international organization that could settle disputes between nations

_____ **21.** The policy of holding back Soviet expansion through nonmilitary and limited military means was known as

   (1) the iron curtain   **(3)** the Berlin blockade
   (2) containment   **(4)** the Warsaw Pact

Base your answer to question 22 on the cartoon below and on your knowledge of social studies.

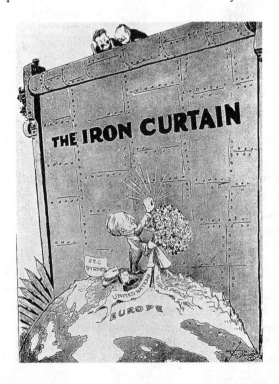

_____ **22.** What does the cartoon say about the attitude of Secretary of State Byrnes toward the Soviet leaders?

(1) He is trying to win them over.
(2) He is ignoring them.
(3) He is angry with them.
(4) He is bored and indifferent to them.

_____ **23.** One proposal in President Truman's Fair Deal program was the

(1) tearing down of public housing
(2) raising of the minimum wage
(3) chartering of the United Nations
(4) creation of a national welfare system

Base your answer to question 24 on the passage below and on your knowledge of social studies.

"I believe that it must be the policy of the United States to support free peoples who are resisting attempted subjugation [conquest] by armed minorities or by outside pressures."

—*President Harry Truman*

_____ **24.** President Truman was committing the United States to providing assistance to countries

(1) whose economies were struggling
(2) who were facing civil war
(3) who were fighting communism
(4) who were joining the Soviet Union

_____ **25.** President Truman ordered federal departments and agencies to

(1) end job discrimination against African Americans
(2) end strikes by labor unions
(3) end job discrimination against Japanese Americans
(4) segregate all federal facilities

Base your answers to questions 26 and 27 on the map below and on your knowledge of social studies.

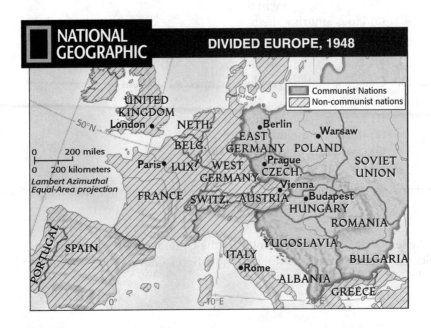

NATIONAL GEOGRAPHIC   **DIVIDED EUROPE, 1948**

Communist Nations
Non-communist nations

_____ 26. What nation was divided into Communist and non-Communist zones?

(1) Poland
(2) France
(3) Austria
(4) Germany

_____ 27. With which Communist countries did Austria share a border?

(1) Yugoslavia, Hungary, and Czechoslovakia
(2) Italy and West Germany
(3) Hungary and Romania
(4) West Germany, East Germany, and Czechoslovakia

_____ 28. What event started the Korean War?

(1) The Soviet Union invaded Korea.   (3) Japan invaded Korea.
(2) South Korea invaded North Korea.   (4) North Korea invaded South Korea.

_____ 29. One result of the Cold War was that

(1) Germany invaded Russia
(2) the United States aided Communist forces
(3) a U.S.-China arms race developed
(4) western nations formed the North Atlantic Treaty Organization

_____ **30.** The domino theory was based on

    (1) the fear of nations falling to communism

    (2) the space race between the United States and the Soviet Union

    (3) a policy of peaceful coexistence between the Soviet Union and the United States

    (4) the fear of foreigners buying land in the United States

_____ **31.** *Sputnik*, the first artificial earth satellite, was

    (1) used as a spy plane

    (2) proof that the Soviets were in an arms race

    (3) launched by the Soviet Union

    (4) the United States' first program to put an astronaut in space

_____ **32.** A measure of people's overall wealth and quality of life is called

    (1) personal income   **(3)** productivity

    (2) standard of living   **(4)** affluence

_____ **33.** Military spending on the Korean War and greater productivity

    (1) helped the U.S. economy grow in the 1950s

    (2) encouraged people to move to the suburbs

    (3) caused the Cold War

    (4) improved prosperity among the rural and urban poor

Base your answer to question 34 on the cartoon below and on your knowledge of social studies.

"I Have Here In My Hand —"

from Herblock's *Here and Now* (Simon & Schuster, 1955)

_____ **34.** Who is the person represented in the cartoon?

    (1) Richard Nixon   **(3)** Julius Rosenberg

    (2) Joseph Welch   **(4)** Joseph McCarthy

Base your answer to question 35 on the flowchart below and on your knowledge of social studies.

_____ **35.** What did Nikita Khrushchev conclude from this series of events?

    (1) Kennedy could not be trusted.

    (2) The U.S. military could not be trusted.

    (3) Kennedy could be bullied.

    (4) Castro could be bullied.

_____ **36.** President Eisenhower thought that if South Vietnam fell to communism, the other countries of Southeast Asia would also fall to communism. This theory was called

    (1) the domino theory   **(3)** the Agent Orange theory

    (2) the Gulf of Tonkin Resolution   **(4)** the credibility gap

_____ **37.** The anthem "We Shall Overcome" is most closely associated with

    (1) the Civil Rights movement

    (2) the Vietnam War

    (3) the women's movement

    (4) the breakup of the Soviet Union

Base your answer to question 38 on the passage below and on your knowledge of social studies.

"The Americans thought that the more bombs they dropped, the quicker we would fall to our knees and surrender. But the bombs heightened, rather than dampened, our spirit."

                                     —*North Vietnamese leader*

————— **38.** What does the quotation say about the North Vietnamese fighters?

(1) They were ready to surrender.
(2) They were scared by the American bombings.
(3) They were determined to defeat the American forces.
(4) They respected American fire power.

————— **39.** Which of the following statements best describes Americans' attitudes toward the Vietnam War?

(1) The longer the war went on, the more support for it decreased.
(2) Support increased as the reasons for the war became clear.
(3) The Tet offensive increased Americans' support of the war.
(4) Most supporters of the war were college students.

————— **40.** How did the Vietnam war end?

(1) The U.S. and South Vietnam won the war.
(2) France won the war.
(3) The Paris peace accords ended the war.
(4) North Vietnam won the war.

————— **41.** Which set of events is in the correct chronological order?

(1) Civil war begins in Vietnam—Gulf of Tonkin Resolution passed—President Nixon sends troops to Cambodia
(2) President Nixon sends troops to Cambodia—civil war begins in Vietnam—Gulf of Tonkin Resolution passed
(3) Gulf of Tonkin Resolution passed—President Nixon sends troops to Cambodia—civil war begins in Vietnam
(4) President Nixon sends troops to Cambodia—Gulf of Tonkin Resolution passed—civil war begins in Vietnam

————— **42.** President Kennedy dealt with two crises involving the Communist threat in

(1) Korea
(2) Vietnam
(3) China
(4) Cuba

————— **43.** Which event began the space race between the United States and the Soviet Union?

(1) Neil Armstrong stepped on the moon.
(2) NASA built a control center.
(3) The Soviets launched *Sputnik*.
(4) Yuri Gagarin orbited the earth.

_____ **44.** The term *coup* refers to

    (1) discrimination against a certain group
    (2) the violent overthrow of a government
    (3) a conflict between two groups in the same country
    (4) ideals worth fighting for

_____ **45.** During the Vietnam War, prowar and antiwar activists were called

    (1) hens and roosters
    (2) cats and dogs
    (3) birds and bees
    (4) hawks and doves

_____ **46.** President Nixon's plan for Vietnamization called for

    (1) establishing a Communist government in South Vietnam
    (2) the invasion of North Vietnam by the Cambodian army
    (3) the army of South Vietnam to take a more active role in fighting
    (4) the United States army to withdraw from Vietnam immediately

_____ **47.** President Nixon's foreign policy plan of détente aimed to

    (1) end the Vietnam war
    (2) stop the spread of communism
    (3) ease tensions between the United States and the Soviet Union as well as China
    (4) drive Palestinians out of Israeli-held territory

Base your answer to question 48 on the cartoon below and on your knowledge of social studies.

Pat Oliphant. *The Denver Post,* 1971.

_____ **48.** What nations do the players represent?

(1) United States, China, and Japan
(2) China, Taiwan, and the United States
(3) North Vietnam, China, and the United States
(4) Japan, Taiwan, and the United States

_____ **49.** How did Arab oil-producing states respond to the United States for supporting Israel?

(1) They refused to accept oil shipments from the United States.
(2) They imposed an embargo of oil shipments to the United States.
(3) They refused to negotiate with Henry Kissinger, the secretary of state.
(4) They overthrew Salvador Allende, the president of Chile.

_____ **50.** What was the end result of the Watergate scandal?

(1) inflation
(2) a budget deficit
(3) President Nixon resigned
(4) an energy crisis

_____ **51.** Which of the following contributed to U.S. economic problems in the 1970s?

(1) Japanese cars not being imported into the United States
(2) European products competing with American-made products
(3) the high prices and limited supply of oil
(4) conflict over the Korean war

Base your answer to question 52 on the events below and on your knowledge of social studies.

A. President Ford vetoes programs in health, housing, and education to reduce government spending
B. Ford pardons Nixon
C. Americans learn CIA and FBI have secret files on citizens

_____ **52.** How did American citizens react to the government actions outlined above?

(1) They were frustrated and angry.
(2) They were supportive of President Ford.
(3) They were occupied with economic issues.
(4) Their trust in government officials increased.

Base your answers to questions 53 and 54 on the table below and on your knowledge of social studies.

GASOLINE CONSUMPTION AND PRICES				
Year	Consumption (Billions of gallons)	Reg.	Prem.	No lead
1973	110.5	$ .40	.45	NA
1974	106.3	.53	.57	.55
1975	109.0	.57	.61	.60
1976	115.7	.59	.64	.61
1977	119.6	.62	.67	.66
1978	125.1	.63	.69	.67
1979	122.1	.86	.92	.90
1980	115.0	1.19	1.28	1.25

Source: *Statistical Abstract of the United States*

53. How much more did a gallon of regular gasoline cost in 1980 than in 1973?

    (1) $0.65
    (2) $0.69
    (3) $0.79
    (4) $0.84

54. Based on billions of gallons of gas consumed, in which year shown on the table was the environment most polluted with automobile fumes?

    (1) 1973
    (2) 1977
    (3) 1978
    (4) 1979

55. Public support for President Carter was seriously damaged by

    (1) the Camp David Accords
    (2) the hostage crisis in Iran
    (3) sanctions against the Soviet Union for invading Afghanistan
    (4) the Strategic Arms Limitation Treaty

Base your answer to question 56 on the passage below and on your knowledge of social studies.

> "It is time for us to realize that we are too great a nation to limit ourselves to small dreams. We're not, as some would have us believe, doomed to an inevitable decline. I do not believe in a fate that will fall on us no matter what we do. I do believe in a fate that will fall on us if we do nothing. . ."
>
> —*from Ronald Reagan's first inaugural address*

_____ 56. Who is the speaker referring to when he says "us"?

(1) Congress
(2) the U.S. government
(3) former presidents of the United States
(4) the American people

_____ 57. Mikhail Gorbachev's plan for reforming the Soviet government was called

(1) glasnost
(2) deregulation
(3) Sovietization
(4) decommunization

Part II: Constructed-Response Questions

DIRECTIONS: *Analyze the image below. Then answer the questions based on the image and on your knowledge of social studies.*

1. Who is the man in the image?

_____

_____

_____

2. What does "our bullets will do it" mean?

_____

_____

_____

3. What was the purpose of this World War II propaganda poster?

_____

_____

_____

DIRECTIONS: *Analyze the cartoon below. Then answer the questions based on the cartoon and on your knowledge of social studies.*

1. Who is the person in the cartoon?

_____

_____

2. What is the cartoon saying about communism?

_____

_____

_____

3. What are some of the countries whose leaders would have been present at this reunion in 1985?

_____

_____

_____

Part III: Document-Based Questions

This exercise is designed to test your ability to work with historical documents. It is similar to the document-based questions that you will see on the Intermediate-Level Test in Social Studies. While you are asked to analyze three historical documents, the exercise on the Intermediate-Level Test in Social Studies may include up to nine documents.

Some of the documents have been edited for the purposes of the question. As you analyze the documents, take into account the source of each document and any point of view that may be presented in the document.

Historical Context: In the second half of the twentieth century, the United States shifted away from isolationism and became increasingly involved in conflicts around the globe. The goal of protecting and promoting democracy is often cited by the United States as the main reason for such involvement.

Task: Use information from the documents and your knowledge of social studies to answer the questions that follow each document in Part A. Then use your answers to help you write the essay in Part B, in which you will be asked to:

> Describe the methods and language U.S. political and military leaders use to encourage or justify involvement in foreign affairs.

Part A: Short-Answer Questions

DIRECTIONS: Analyze the documents and answer the questions that follow each document in the space provided. Your answers to the questions will help you write the essay.

Document 1 President John F. Kennedy, on October 22, 1962, explaining to the U.S. and Cuban people what steps the U.S. government would take in reaction to the Soviet Union placing medium-range missiles in Cuba

> Many times in the past, the Cuban people have risen to throw out tyrants who destroyed their liberty. And I have no doubt that most Cubans today look forward to the time when they will be truly free from foreign domination, free to choose their own leaders, free to select their own system, free to own their own land, free to speak and write and worship without fear or degradation. And then shall Cuba be welcomed back to the society of free nations and to the association of nations of this hemisphere. . . . The path we have chosen for the present is full of hazards, as all paths are; but it is the one most consistent with our character and courage as a nation and our commitments around the world. The cost of freedom is always high—but Americans have always paid it. And one path we shall never choose, and that is the path of surrender or submission.

1._a_ Why do you think President Kennedy reminds the Cuban people that, in the past, Cubans have risen up to overthrow their leaders?

_____

_____

_b_ According to President Kennedy, when will Cuba be welcomed into the association of nations of the Western Hemisphere?

_____

_____

Document 2 Secretary of State John Foster Dulles, speaking before the U.S. Senate in 1953

> We shall never have a secure peace or a happy world so long as Soviet Communism dominates one-third of all of the peoples that there are, and is in the process of trying at least to extend its rule to many others. These people who are enslaved are people who deserve to be free, and who, from our own selfish standpoint, ought to be free. . . . [W]e must always have in mind the liberation of these captive peoples. Now, liberation does not mean a war of liberation. Liberation can be accomplished by processes short of war. . . . It must be and can be a peaceful process, but those who do not believe that results can be accomplished by moral pressures, by the weight of propaganda, just do not know what they are talking about. I ask you to recall the fact that Soviet Communism, itself, has spread from controlling 200 million people some seven years ago to controlling 800 million people today, and it has done that by methods of political warfare, psychological warfare and propaganda, and it has not actually used the Red Army as an open aggressive force in accomplishing that.

2._a_ According to Dulles, why did the United States need to address the issue of Soviet expansion in Europe?

_____

_____

_b_ What Soviet methods did Dulles believe the United States should imitate to accomplish peaceful "liberation" of people living under Soviet rule?

_____

_____

Document 3 President George W. Bush, announcing on May 1, 2003, that major combat in Iraq has ended and Saddam Hussein is no longer the leader of Iraq

> In this battle, we have fought for the cause of liberty and for the peace of the world. Our nation and our coalition are proud of this accomplishment—yet, it is you, the members of the United States military, who achieved it. Your courage, your willingness to face danger for your country and for each other, made this day possible. Because of you, our nation is more secure. Because of you, the tyrant has fallen, and Iraq is free. . . . In the images of celebrating Iraqis, we have also seen the ageless appeal of human freedom. Decades of lies and intimidation could not make the Iraqi people love their oppressors or desire their own enslavement. Men and women in every culture need liberty like they need food and water and air. Everywhere that freedom arrives, humanity rejoices; and everywhere that freedom stirs, let tyrants fear.

3.　What does Bush imply when he says, "Everywhere that freedom stirs, let tyrants fear"?

_____

_____

Part B: Essay

DIRECTIONS: *Write a well-organized essay that includes an introduction, several paragraphs, and a conclusion. Use evidence from the three documents in the body of the essay. Support your response with relevant facts, examples, and details. Include additional outside information.*

> Describe the methods and language U.S. political and military leaders use to encourage or justify involvement in foreign affairs.

Unit 11—The American People in a Changing World, *1950–Present*

Overview

By the 1950s, African American leaders were ready to challenge segregation. In 1954 the Supreme Court unanimously ruled that separate schools were unconstitutional, but it was a long battle to integrate schools across the nation. In Montgomery, Alabama, Rosa Parks was arrested for refusing to give up her seat on the bus to a white man. The bus boycott that followed lasted for more than a year, until the bus segregation law was also ruled unconstitutional.

In 1960 John Kennedy was elected president of the United States. His plans included guaranteeing civil rights for all Americans. But in 1963, Kennedy was shot and killed. President Lyndon Johnson introduced even more proposals with his Great Society programs. Through the early 1960s, many different groups organized efforts to gain equality for African Americans. Many of these efforts were met with violence, but many gains were made.

By 1974 it was evident that Nixon had taken part in illegal activities and their cover-up. Faced with impeachment, the president resigned. Vice President Gerald Ford became president.

In 1992, Bill Clinton was elected president. He succeeded in cutting the national debt and running a budget surplus. Faced with scandals involving the president, the House of Representatives voted to impeach him. In the Senate trial, the president was found not guilty.

President George W. Bush soon faced his first crisis. On September 11, 2001, two hijacked passenger airplanes were flown into the World Trade Center in New York City. Another crashed into the Pentagon. On a fourth hijacked plane, passengers heroically attacked the hijackers, causing the plane to crash into an open field. President Bush established a new department, Homeland Security, and organized a war on terrorism. The effort to protect Americans continued when the U.S. military attacked Iraq in March 2003. President Bush argued that the Iraqis were hiding weapons of mass destruction. Even after the regime of Iraqi dictator Saddam Hussein was toppled, it was clear that the path toward a stable Iraq would not be quick or easy.

Essential Questions

As you prepare for the Intermediate-Level Test in Social Studies, ask yourself these essential questions:

- What were the major events in the civil rights movement?
- What effect did the Watergate scandal have on politics?
- What events led to President Clinton's impeachment?
- How has the United States responded to the threat of terrorism?

Part I: Multiple-Choice Questions

DIRECTIONS: Write the number of the answer that best completes the statement or answers the question.

_____   1.   As more people and businesses moved to the suburbs in the 1950s, American cities

(1) faced growing problems with poverty and crime
(2) prospered
(3) experienced job growth
(4) became more materialistic

Base your answer to question 2 on the line graph below and on your knowledge of social studies.

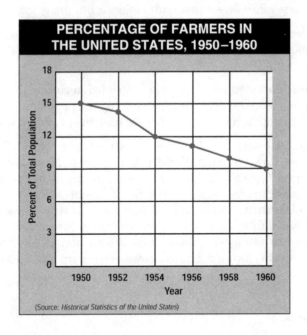

PERCENTAGE OF FARMERS IN THE UNITED STATES, 1950–1960

(Source: *Historical Statistics of the United States*)

_____   2.   What percentage of Americans were farmers in 1954?

(1) 12 percent   (3) 15 percent
(2) 11 percent   (4) 9 percent

_____   3.   Which of the following was developed by Jonas Salk?

(1) automation
(2) the National Aeronautics and Space Administration
(3) television advertising
(4) a polio vaccine

_____ **4.** The Supreme Court decision in *Brown* v. *Board of Education of Topeka*
(1) criticized the lack of individuality in middle-class, suburban schools
(2) declared racial segregation in public schools to be unconstitutional
(3) criticized the quality of public schools in cities
(4) criticized the effects of television on children

_____ **5.** Civil disobedience is
(1) the refusal to obey laws that are considered unjust
(2) the refusal to attend public schools
(3) the refusal to obey city laws
(4) the refusal to use public transportation

_____ **6.** The arrest of Rosa Parks resulted in the boycott of
(1) restaurants   (3) public schools
(2) buses   (4) motels

Base your answer to question 7 on the time line below and on your knowledge of social studies.

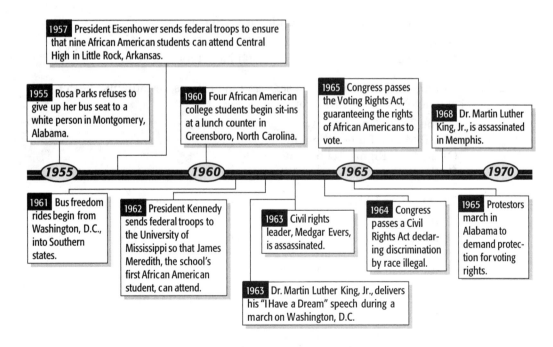

_____ **7.** When did Dr. Martin Luther King, Jr., deliver his "I Have a Dream" speech?
(1) 1961   (3) 1963
(2) 1962   (4) 1964

_____ 8. Dr. Martin Luther King, Jr., was influenced by the nonviolent ideas of

   (1) Orval Faubus
   (2) Thurgood Marshall
   (3) Malcolm X
   (4) Mohandas Gandhi

Base your answer to question 9 on the events below and on your knowledge of social studies.

   A. 1962: James Meredith enrolls at University of Mississippi
   B. 1967: Thurgood Marshall appointed to Supreme Court
   C. 1968: Shirley Chisholm elected to House of Representatives
   D. 1972: Barbara Jordan elected to Congress

_____ 9. The events above are all a result of

   (1) segregation
   (2) the civil rights movement
   (3) the assassination of Dr. Martin Luther King, Jr.
   (4) the foundation of Southern Christian Leadership Council

_____ 10. President Johnson's administration is known as the

   (1) war on poverty   **(3)** New Deal
   (2) Great Society   **(4)** New Frontier

_____ 11. Discrimination in hiring and segregation in stores, restaurants, theaters, and hotels were outlawed by

   (1) the Black Panther Party
   (2) Dr. Martin Luther King, Jr.
   (3) the Civil Rights Act of 1964
   (4) the Voting Rights Act of 1965

_____ 12. The Freedom Riders tested the enforcement of

   (1) the Voting Rights Act of 1965
   (2) a Supreme Court ruling that made segregation of bus facilities illegal
   (3) the Civil Rights Act of 1964
   (4) the Equal Rights Amendment

_____ 13. How did the idea of Black Power differ from Martin Luther King's goals for the civil rights movement?

   (1) Black Power was a peaceful movement; King's was not.
   (2) King advocated non-violence; Black Power supporters were not opposed to violence.
   (3) Black Power wanted integration into white society; King did not.
   (4) King advocated African Americans' return to Africa; Black Power supporters did not.

_____ **14.** The Indian Civil Rights Act of 1968

    (1) established the American Indian Movement
    (2) prevented Native Americans from riding on city buses
    (3) allowed Native Americans to live on reservations
    (4) protected Native Americans' constitutional rights

_____ **15.** A major goal of the National Organization for Women was

    (1) a repeal of the Equal Pay Act
    (2) increasing Americans' materialism
    (3) allowing women to retire at a younger age than men
    (4) adding an Equal Rights Amendment to the Constitution

_____ **16.** Consumers supported the United Farm Workers union by

    (1) buying farm produce only from Hispanic Americans
    (2) refusing to buy boycotted farm produce
    (3) going on Freedom Rides
    (4) supporting voting rights for Hispanic Americans

_____ **17.** President Kennedy's Alliance for Progress promoted

    (1) equal pay for women
    (2) growth in Latin America
    (3) desegregation in southern states
    (4) the formation of the Green Berets

_____ **18.** César Chávez is most closely associated with

    (1) the United Farm Workers
    (2) the League of Latin American Citizens
    (3) the National Congress of American Indians
    (4) La Raza Unida

_____ **19.** Why did President Kennedy create the Peace Corps?

    (1) to support third world countries
    (2) to provide economic incentives to Latin America
    (3) to counteract the appeal of communism
    (4) to provide American youth with a service program

_____ **20.** Which of the following events took place years after the other three?

    (1) Martin Luther King, Jr., was assassinated.
    (2) Robert Kennedy was assassinated.
    (3) Richard Nixon resigned from office.
    (4) Violence marred the Democratic National Convention.

_____ **21.** Which event sparked the student unrest at Kent State University?

    (1) the draft of National Guard troops

    (2) the invasion of Cambodia

    (3) the withdrawal of American troops from Vietnam

    (4) a change in the selective service system

_____ **22.** The term *affirmative action* refers to

    (1) giving increased aid to public schools

    (2) giving minority applicants preference in jobs

    (3) attacking social problems in a positive way

    (4) contributing to political campaign funds

Base your answer to question 23 on the graph below and on your knowledge of social studies.

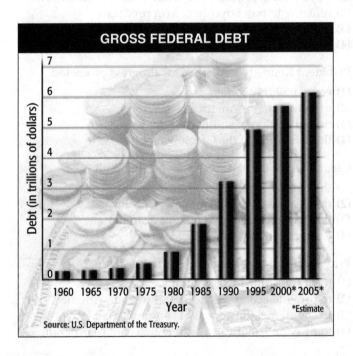

Source: U.S. Department of the Treasury.

_____ **23.** When did the gross federal debt first pass $1 trillion?

    (1) 1985

    (2) 1990

    (3) 1995

    (4) 2000

———— **24.** What happened in the Iran-Contra scandal?

    (1) The United States secretly sold weapons to Iran and used the money to fight Nicaraguan rebels known as contras.

    (2) The United States secretly sold weapons to Iran in exchange for help in freeing American hostages, then used the money to help anticommunist rebels in Nicaragua known as contras.

    (3) Iran stole weapons from the United States and sent them to anticommunist rebels in Nicaragua known as contras.

    (4) Nicaraguan fighters known as contras bought weapons from Iran and used them to take American hostages.

Base your answer to question 25 on the time line below and on your knowledge of social studies.

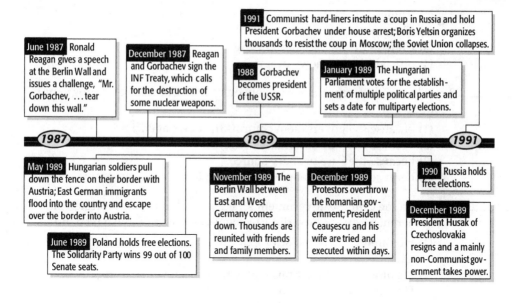

———— **25.** When did Russia hold free elections for the first time?

    (1) 1987

    (2) 1988

    (3) 1989

    (4) 1990

———— **26.** How did the fall of communism in Eastern Europe affect Germany?

    (1) Germany constructed a new Berlin Wall.

    (2) Germany became a republic of the Soviet Union.

    (3) Germany became reunited as a democratic country.

    (4) Germany became reunited as a communist country.

Base your answers to questions 27 and 28 on the excerpt below and on your knowledge of social studies.

> "The official news programs this morning reported that the People's Liberation Army had crushed a 'counter-revolutionary rebellion' in the capital. They said that more than 1,000 police and troops had been injured and some killed, and that civilians had been killed, but did not give details. . . .
>
> The announcement by the Beijing news program suggested that Prime Minister Li Peng, who is backed by hard-liners in the Communist Party, was still on top in his power struggle for control of the Chinese leadership."
> —*from* The New York Times, *June 4, 1989*

_____ 27. What sources does the reporter cite?

(1) Chinese doctors
(2) Chinese citizens
(3) Chinese Prime Minister Li Peng
(4) official Chinese news programs

_____ 28. Why would a report based solely on official Chinese news programs be doubted?

(1) because the government controls the news agencies
(2) because they are secondary sources
(3) because they are primary sources
(4) because multiple people contributed to the news programs

_____ 29. When the Chinese government killed several hundred protesters in Tiananmen Square, how did President George H.W. Bush respond?

(1) He carefully avoided strong disapproval that might affect trade with China.
(2) He broke off all relations with China to show his disapproval.
(3) He sent troops to China.
(4) He strongly supported the Chinese government.

_____ 30. Which of the following increased public approval of President George H.W. Bush?

(1) his refusal to involve the federal government in stimulating the economy
(2) the failure of many savings and loan associations
(3) the recession
(4) Operation Desert Storm

Base your answers to questions 31 and 32 on the map below and on your knowledge of social studies.

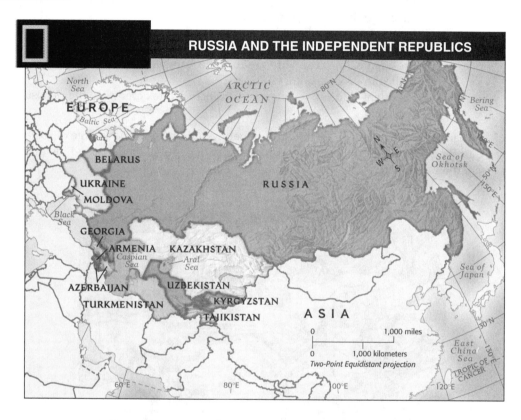

RUSSIA AND THE INDEPENDENT REPUBLICS

_____ **31.** Which republics border Belarus?

    (1) Ukraine and Europe   **(3)** Russia and Ukraine

    (2) Armenia and Georgia   **(4)** Russia and Moldova

_____ **32.** Which of the republics have the best access to shipping lanes in the Black Sea?

    (1) Russia, Georgia, and Ukraine

    (2) Armenia, Azerbaijan, and Turkmenistan

    (3) Russia and Europe

    (4) Kazakhstan and Uzbekistan

_____ **33.** What economic issues reduced President George H.W. Bush's popularity?

    (1) increased federal spending and higher taxes

    (2) eased banking regulations

    (3) savings and loans failures, high levels of debts and bankruptcy

    (4) reduction of the federal debt and increased government spending

_____ 34. Which of the following statements is true?

(1) President Clinton failed in passing a law that imposed background checks for handgun purchases.

(2) Congress thought President Clinton's health-care reform plan was too reliant on government control.

(3) President Clinton aimed to reduce the number of Americans covered by health-care insurance.

(4) President Clinton's economic plan included tax credits to the richest Americans.

Base your answer to question 35 on the cartoon below and on your knowledge of social studies. Cartoonists often use the elephant to represent the Republican Party and the donkey to represent the Democratic Party.

HENG
LIANHE ZAOBAO
SINGAPORE

_____ 35. What statement is the cartoonist making about Congress and the president?

(1) President Clinton would have an easy time passing his programs with a Republican Congress.

(2) President Clinton got along well with Republicans in Congress.

(3) President Clinton would have difficulty moving his programs through a Republican Congress.

(4) President Clinton felt comfortable dealing with the Republicans.

36. Which of the following statements about President Clinton is true?

(1) He was impeached but found to be not guilty of any crimes.

(2) He was impeached and removed from office for his crimes.

(3) He was found guilty of perjury but innocent of obstruction of justice.

(4) He was found not guilty of any crimes but failed to win reelection.

37. Under the North American Free Trade Agreement (NAFTA)

(1) the United States, Canada, and Mexico agreed to eliminate trade barriers among the three nations

(2) Canada and Mexico agreed not to do business with the United States

(3) the United States, Canada, and Mexico agreed to fight communism in North America

(4) the nations of North America agreed not to do business with the nations of South America

38. In the presidential election of 2000, a manual recount of votes took place in

(1) Texas

(2) New York

(3) California

(4) Florida

39. The authorization of force against Iraq was based on the belief that

(1) Osama bin Laden was hiding in Iraq

(2) Iraq had a large store of weapons of mass destruction

(3) Iraq was responsible for the terrorist attack on the United States

(4) Saddam Hussein was planning on invading Kuwait

40. Federal prosecutors and FBI agents were given new powers to investigate terrorism by which of the following?

(1) the Taliban

(2) the USA Patriot Act of 2001

(3) the Powell Doctrine

(4) the World Trade Organization

Part II: Constructed-Response Questions

DIRECTIONS: *Analyze the graph below. Then answer the questions based on the graph and on your knowledge of social studies.*

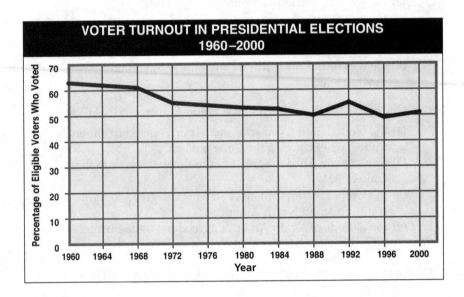

1. Look at the voter turnout percentages for the years 1968 and 2000. How many more voters turned out in 1968 than in 2000?

_____

_____

_____

2. What year had the lowest voter turnout?

_____

_____

_____

3. What trend in voter turnout does the graph show?

_____

_____

_____

DIRECTIONS: Read the passage below. Then answer the questions based on the passage and on your knowledge of social studies.

> In far too many ways American Negroes have been another nation: deprived of freedom, crippled by hatred, the doors of opportunity closed to hope. In our time change has come to this Nation too. The American Negro, acting with impressive restraint, has peacefully protested and marched, entered the courtrooms and the seats of government, demanding a justice that has long been denied. The voice of the Negro was the call to action. But it is a tribute to America that, once aroused, the courts and the Congress, the President and most of the people, have been the allies of progress.
> —*President Lyndon B. Johnson, speaking on June 4, 1965,*
> *about inequality and African Americans*

1. What did Johnson mean when he said that African Americans had been "another nation"?

   _____

   _____

   _____

2. What methods did African Americans use to demand equality?

   _____

   _____

   _____

3. Did Johnson think that the people of the United States responded well to African Americans' demands for equality? How can you tell?

   _____

   _____

   _____

Part III: Document-Based Questions

This exercise is designed to test your ability to work with historical documents. It is similar to the document-based questions that you will see on the Intermediate-Level Test in Social Studies. While you are asked to analyze three historical documents, the exercise on the Intermediate-Level Test in Social Studies may include up to nine documents.

Some of the documents have been edited for the purposes of the question. As you analyze the documents, take into account the source of each document and any point of view that may be presented in the document.

Historical Context: From the time of America's earliest settlers to the twenty-first century, brave men and women have taken—and continue to take—extraordinary risks to blaze new trails.

Task: Use information from the documents and your knowledge of social studies to answer the questions that follow each document in Part A. Then use your answers to help you write the essay in Part B, in which you will be asked to:

> Describe the reasons that Americans have taken—and continue to take—
> extraordinary risks to explore new places. Discuss how advances in technology
> have both increased and limited the risks of explorers.

Part A: Short-Answer Questions

DIRECTIONS: Analyze the documents and answer the questions that follow each document in the space provided. Your answers to the questions will help you write the essay.

Document 1 Frenchman Samuel de Champlain was exploring Canadian America with a band of Huron Indians around 1608 when he became lost in the woods—a major risk in the largely unexplored New World. Fortunately he found his way back to the Huron, who had been searching for him.

> When they first went out hunting, I lost my way in the woods, having
> followed a certain bird that seemed to me peculiar. . . . The night was coming
> on, I was obliged to spend it at the foot of a great tree, and in the morning set
> out and walked until three o'clock in the afternoon, when I came to little pond
> of still water. . . .
>
> When I had made my repast I began to consider what I should do, and to
> pray God to give me the will and courage to sustain patiently my misfortune if
> I should be obliged to remain abandoned in this forest. . . . Thus committing to
> his mercy I gathered up renewed courage, going here and there all day, with-
> out perceiving any foot-print or path, except for wild beast, of which I general-
> ly saw a good number. . . . Unfortunately I had forgotten to bring with me a
> small compass which would have put me on the right road, or nearly so. . . .

1.*a* What misfortunes might de Champlain have experienced if he had not found his way?

_____

_____

b Why did de Champlain pray for "will and courage"?

_____

_____

c What mistake did de Champlain make?

_____

_____

Document 2 What drives people to explore? *National Geographic* magazine sought to answer that question. Reporter Priit J. Vesilind collected some thoughts on the motives behind exploration and presented them in the February 1998 issue of the magazine.

> We are a dim and lonely star in the darkness of the deep-sea floor, where no other light has shone. I am on my belly in a submarine, 2,800 feet down—where the water pressure would crush the lungs of an unprotected human being—peering through a porthole. . . .
>
> As I watch through the porthole, we reach the remains of a Roman-era cargo ship: silt-covered piles of amphorae—graceful clay pots for shipping wine or oil—copper kettles, an anchor. . . . Archaeological exploration has never been attempted this deep, on such a scale, and with such a multidisciplinary team. . . .
>
> [Team leader Robert Ballard] describes his work as a series of quests, like the ones undertaken by the original Jason in pursuit of the Golden Fleece.
>
> "Exploration is still the epic journey," he said, "to dream, to prepare yourself, to assemble your team of argonauts, to go forth to be tested mentally and physically by the gods. To pass the test, to be given the truth, and then come back and share the new wisdom."
>
> For Ballard the spirit of exploration is an integral part of being human.

2.*a* Where is the expedition described in the excerpt taking place?

_____

_____

b What does the excerpt say about why humans are driven to explore?

_____

_____

c How does the author feel about exploration? How do you know?

_____

_____

Document 3 John Noble Wilford, space reporter for the *New York Times*, writing in reaction to the *Challenger* space shuttle disaster that took place on January 28, 1986

> . . . Today the almost casual acceptance of technology exploded in a fireball. And suddenly, as a result, people are jolted into realizing once again the extreme vulnerabilities that all humans must inevitably subject themselves to when they attempt exploration, or even when they are simply willing to place their fates in the hands of technology.
>
> The recent space flights were beginning to seem so matter-of-fact that the television networks ceased their live coverage of launchings and landings. Newspaper accounts were often relegated to the inside pages. The shuttles went up, and life went on with hardly a passing glance. . . .
>
> At times like these, the nation is shaken into a reappraisal of the bargain modern society makes in relying so much on advanced technologies. It has known these moments before. . . .
>
> Still, there is no going back. The world's dependence on technology makes that impossible, and, it seems in the end, there is an enduring optimism that technology's benefits generally outweigh its ill effects and the disastrous moments that seem to make it undesirable.
>
> The shuttles will no doubt fly again. . . . Americans will again put their trust in this bold new technology. Astronauts will fly the shuttles again because it is their calling, and they believe in what they are doing. Others, including journalists, will probably venture into space, too, no doubt approaching the adventure with a new respect, and some dread, with the image of the *Challenger* fireball in mind forever.

3.*a* What happened to the *Challenger* space shuttle?

_____

_____

_____

b What does Wilford mean when he says that modern society makes a "bargain with technologies"?

_____

_____

_____

c What is Wilford's opinion about new technologies? How do you know?

_____

_____

_____

Part B: Essay

DIRECTIONS: *Write a well-organized essay that includes an introduction, several paragraphs, and a conclusion. Use evidence from the three documents in the body of the essay. Support your response with relevant facts, examples, and details. Include additional outside information.*

> Describe the reasons that Americans have taken—and continue to take—extraordinary risks to explore new places. Discuss how advances in technology have both increased and limited the risks of explorers.